THE MANUAL

A RAPID RELIEF FROM EMOTIONAL DISTRESS

REVISED 2022

James E. Campbell M.D.

Copyright © 2022 James E. Campbell M.D.

All rights reserved. No part of this book may be reproduced, stored, or transmitted by any means—whether auditory, graphic, mechanical, or electronic—without written permission of both publisher and author, except in the case of brief excerpts used in critical articles and reviews. Unauthorized reproduction of any part of this work is illegal and is punishable by law.

ISBN: 979-8-88640-376-3 (sc)
ISBN: 979-8-88640-377-0 (hc)
ISBN: 979-8-88640-378-7 (e)

Because of the dynamic nature of the Internet, any web addresses or links contained in this book may have changed since publication and may no longer be valid. The views expressed in this work are solely those of the author and do not necessarily reflect the views of the publisher, and the publisher hereby disclaims any responsibility for them.

One Galleria Blvd., Suite 1900, Metairie, LA 70001
1-888-421-2397

Change		Really		Mental
	Is		for	
Thinking		Bad		Health

Dedicated to all my patients over the years
that have allowed me to practice on them, who have
shown me when I was doing something useful by
getting better, and who have insisted
I get it right by returning.

INTRODUCTION

I rewrite aspects of the book because with time comes further insights. I wanted the size of the book itself to reflect rapid relief. If I look at book on rapid relief over 150 pages long I think it might take me too long just to read the book. I refer to individuals I work with by the time-tested designation of patient. The reference does not in any way intend to demean anyone, or exalt anyone, but is a reflection of the very special bond doctor and patient have enjoyed since the birth of medicine, and which managed care has done it's best to destroy.

Disclaimer: I do not have the backing of any large drug company grant or university setting and therefore my fifty plus years of treating patients may not be seen by some as leading to any scientific, or as we say now "Evidence Based," conclusions. I have some real concerns about the direction that psychiatry as a field has gone over the past 15-20 years. My initial training in psychiatry was in a psychoanalytic program (Michael Reese in Chicago). Very little medication was used to treat patients in that setting. Now, I see almost all people being treated with medicine, and very few are treated with therapy. Some residency programs do not even teach therapy. The managed care entities contributed to that by not being willing to pay psychiatrists to do psychotherapy. The result is a lot of people are on medications that probably do not need them.

When I entered the real world, I was not prepared by my training to treat the many patients who did need medicine. Then, I found a form of therapy that actually reduced my need to use medications by nearly half, or more. Currently, I see people being severely over treated for conditions described as metabolic, or medical, that I routinely treat using brief psychotherapy interventions. In the fifty years I have been in practice I have seen the pendulum swing from one extreme to another; I like neither.

Since it was first published, people have commented to me about the book, and I was happy with how often they commented positively.

HOW TO GET RAPID RELIEF

If you suffer from hurt, dissatisfaction, jealousy, frustration, resentment, helplessness, hopelessness demoralization, anger, guilt, shame, anxiety, depression or are distressed over work, love, money, health, and a host of other problem, you are one of the walking wounded. You may be able to get up each day, eat breakfast, go to work, come home, eat dinner, and go to bed, but you're in pain. If you would like to learn the necessary steps to get rid of the pain related to these life issues keep reading.

You may believe you need something to change in order to get relief ("I need to have my job back"; "I need her to love me"; "I need to get myself to stop drinking"), but actually it's your "need" to change reality that causes your pain. Remove this "need" for self, situation or other to be different" and you eliminate the pain.

How you love, work, and play depends on whether you operate from a system focused on the <u>need</u> for self, situation or others to be different or from a system where you <u>create</u> what you want by means of choice, movement, or selection. Let go of the belief you must change yourself, others, or the world, and you will eliminate much of your stress and distress. Once you decide to design your life by choice, you make a quantum leap into a richer, more satisfying life.

Rapid relief is possible! Psychological pain is optional!

Most people have major life problems: divorces, bankruptcies, deaths of loved ones, failed hopes and dreams. How quickly one switches out of their distress isn't related to the perceived magnitude of their life problem, but rather to how quickly they can get into a state of acceptance, and out of a state of need. Getting out of need does not solve the life problem immediately, but it does stop the psychological pain.

Some people with major losses (e.g., the death of a spouse) can eliminate their distress relatively quickly; others with minor problems (a job they dislike) may take longer. But no matter what is seen as the cause of emotional distress, once we begin to create our lives by becoming aware of options and making choices, we get relief from the psychological pain.

When I served as a psychiatrist for the Air Force in Puerto Rico, I had a glimpse of the possibility of rapid relief for some conditions. In my psychiatric residency at Michael Reese Hospital in Chicago, I had treated the same patients for one, two, or three years. In the Air Force, however, there was a need to make rapid decisions about a person's condition, and to provide a quick treatment for problem so the service man could get back to work.

During this assignment I had a rapid recovery from an airman. For three consecutive nights he had been treated for panic attacks in the emergency room of the base hospital. On the fourth morning I received a call from the chief of the medical unit; they wanted me to work this airman into my schedule, because the nightly panic attacks were disrupting his work. I was booked solid that day, so could give him only a few minutes between appointments.

I skipped the formal psychiatric interview when he came in and simply asked what was bothering him. He said he felt extremely uncomfortable working indoors; I pulled out a prescription pad and wrote on it that he was to be given an outdoor job for the time being, and then I made an appointment to see him at the next available time.

When I did see him again, he was doing fine. After seeing the prescription, the airman's commanding officer had given him a job outside for a few days. Later, the officer asked the airman to work inside again, where he was greatly needed. He was given the option of returning outside, if he felt panicked again. The airman agreed and returned to his regular job where he was able to work without difficulty. Becoming aware of his choices (to work indoors or outdoors) enabled him to accept the situation and make a choice (to work indoors). He stopped trying to control his anxiety, which actually escalated it, and made a different choice instead; his panic attacks stopped.

If I had used Ativan, or Xanax, I would have felt they were responsible for his rapid recovery. More accurately, what helped him was the same event that caused the issue in the first place: the cognitive bombshell of "have to." Over time "have to" has become more, and more, important to me as a cause of psychiatric disorders. Subconsciously, this, and other similar events, created for me a conceptual challenge as to what constitutes a "mental illness," and how it should be approached therapeutically. Is this type of symptom deserving of a mental health diagnosis, or is it simply a normal product of a particular way of thinking? When the thinking is altered, it alters the symptom.

Rapid relief from emotional distress is possible, because both the distress and the relief come from within. Events, and people, don't cause your psychological world of experience, or feelings. When you let events, or other people, determine your psychological world, you will always be shoved around by those forces. In that thinking to feel good, you will either have to struggle to change people, change external and internal events, or be stuck waiting for them to change. You could be miserable for the rest of your life, because many events in your life can never be changed. Understanding you have a choice to create and expand your life, you'll begin to feel relief. The only energy you need to expend is the energy to stay alert to the choices you have. No matter how bad you feel 0(psychologically) right now; you have the key to relief in your mind.

Seven steps to Immediate Relief:

1. Understand you create your psychological pain.
2. Understand the difference between change and choice.
3. Use the ACT Formula. (Discussed on page 7)
4. Be precise in your language.

5. Use critical opportunities to increase your skill at making choices.
6. Understand the difference between cause and effect and sequential ordering of events.
7. Be aware how physical and psychological worlds work with different principles, and how they have different languages associated with them.

Know that you create your psychological pain

This may cause some consternation, but please keep reading! Sometimes at this point people will want to debate about what is true. Is it true we create our own psychological pain? The truthful answer is, "I don't know." What I do know for certain is that accepting the belief that we create our own thoughts, feelings and actions, makes a major difference in the bottom line (our life experience). It is like the debate about free will. No one can prove if there is free will. What we know is that the lives of people who believe in free will are very different from those who do not believe in free will. A similar thing can be said about the belief in an afterlife, in God, etc. The difference in our beliefs appears sometimes to be culturally determined. In the United States we have a proverb: "Sticks and stones may break my bones, but words will never hurt me." This reflects the point of view that words do not have power in them to cause injury. In India there is a proverb, "The wounds from sticks and stones will heal, but those from words may never heal." This reflects the point of view that it is words that have the most power to harm a person. Look closely at the countries that have this philosophy, and then look at how many years they have been at war with their neighbors. Listen to the commentaries on what the disagreements are between them, and see if you can pick up the form of the proverb they are practicing. The current administration has chosen to move the United States into the path of the second proverb.

The first step toward rapid relief is to realize what you are doing to create your pain. Part of our emotional pain is a product of a blame way of thinking. We often experience this in the form of an idea that "Others (or events) need to change, because they are responsible for our thoughts, feelings, and actions," and that "I need to be on a constant lookout, because I am responsible for others' thoughts, feelings, and actions."

When you are caught up in this belief system (a blame system), you will experience one, or more, of the following inevitable & unpleasant emotional reactions:

1. Hurt—"Why did they have to say that to me?"
2. Dissatisfaction—"Life is not worth living when you feel like I do!"
3. Disapproval—"You could have done better, if you had only tried."
4. Jealousy—"You were so busy thinking about them, you forgot my wishes."
5. Waiting –"They have to change, before I can feel better."
6. Frustration—"Why don't they change?"
7. Helplessness—"I can't change my feelings."
8. Hopelessness—"You can't help me do better."
9. Resentment—"I hate them for making me feel this way."
10. Sense of Failure—"I try, but I can't make it different."
11. Demoralization—"No one seems able to help me."
12. Depression—"I should be able to make them change; I can't change them, so I'm a loser." (Ranges from helpless to rage)
13. Superficial Communication—"I can't say what I want; because, if I do, I'll hurt someone's feelings."
14. Intimacy issues—"I try to be independent and avoid everyone, but then I feel cut off, vulnerable, and lonely." (Getting close *makes, me* vulnerable; it is best that I stay away.)
15. Failure to develop a good sense of self—"Because I let outside events and people determine my life, I don't know who, or what, I am. I am not in touch with myself, or my own needs."

The products of this belief system are listed somewhat in progression from the least to the most troublesome. People often follow them in the order listed. Waiting and hurt ("My husband shouldn't have done that") can fall all the way into a clinical depression ("Nobody loves me; my life is one failure after another."). These feelings are eliminated once you get out of the blame system of thinking. Stop your efforts to change something, and, instead, start making choices that will get you what you want.

Know the difference between change and choice

In the choice system you understand: "I'm responsible for my thoughts, feelings, and actions; others are responsible for their thoughts, feelings, and actions."

By responsibility, I mean our ability to create (respond to) and manage our own thoughts, feelings, and actions. In the choice system, you maintain accountable for all of your thoughts, feelings and actions, because you recognize you create them, either directly, or indirectly. When you stay accountable and understand responsibility in your life, you become the primary creative force in your life. Because your choices create your experiences, you can create a huge variety of experiences by making new choices. {It is sometimes not appreciated that we really do not live in a change world; we actually live in a creation world. Today, through the choices we are making, we create the experience we will have tomorrow, and the tomorrows after that.}

Choice is not another name for change. Change is a concept best applied to the physical world; change may be very difficult to accomplish. It typically takes time ("I can't change overnight"), energy ("I am just too tired"), and special knowledge ("Someone will have to teach me how to do this"). Once the task of change is accomplished, the results are something totally different from the original. The new product is expected to remain permanent and stable ("Once I change, I will live happily all the rest of my life"). Because change takes so much time and energy, there is a natural tendency to resist it at the psychological level ("It's hopeless, I'll never change").

Choice, on the other hand, is simple. The only energy you need to spend is the amount required to stay aware of the current options you have available to select from. Choice is a basic psychological process, and is simple to do. You don't need any tools; selecting among options requires little, or no time. Choice, unlike change, doesn't result in a stable result. Making choices that lead to happiness doesn't mean your continued happiness is insured. Choice usually leaves you with the same options you started with –nothing has changed—but the outcome is different with each different selection one makes (we put unused choices back on the "table of options").

When you focus on creating something, rather than on trying to change something, there are immediate results. Creating what you want in life also generates positive feelings:

1. Acceptance—"I can accept reality, because my happiness and creativity aren't dependent on events, or others, being different."
2. Energy—"I can do something right now to create the experiences I want, because it does not take a lot of energy."
3. Knowledge—"I can learn something from any situation."
4. Resourcefulness—"By looking at the current reality, I can find choices I can use."
5. Cooperation—"I can collaborate with others, so we all get some of what we want."
6. Success—"Success is dependent on the quality of the selections one makes. Sometimes the best choice is not the first one. Studies show one attribute of successful people that seems consistent: Successful people take more time making decisions than others do."
7. Self-esteem—"Self-esteem follows the development of, and the understanding of what it takes to make ones' self happy."
8. Honest Communication—"When I tell the truth to myself and others, I build up my self-esteem, and I will generally influence others esteem at the same time."
9. Intimacy—"Intimacy is extremely difficult to achieve in the blame system, because of the sense of vulnerability that is a part of that system. Only in a system where individuals accept they create their own feelings can we get close without putting up defensive barriers. When I understand and accept that you (other) are not responsible for my feelings, I have the choice to be as close to you

as I want. I can be myself, and if I'm not trying to change you and you can be yourself."
10. A Good Sense of Self—"This is a product of building self-esteem over time. The more we understand what makes us happy, and the more we do those things that make us happy, the better is our sense of self in general. There is a catch 22 here. Individuals who have character disorders (some alcoholics, most drug users, child molesters, wife abusers) do what they do, because they like what they are doing. They like the effect of the chemical or the feeling of power over others. When you work with these individuals, as I do, you do not see good self-esteem. There is absolute failure in these individuals to achieve other esteem."

As you broaden your ability to make choices, you will find you automatically have more positive experiences in your life.

Are you in change, or choice, thinking? At this moment, I bet, you are either trying to change yourself, or you are making choices that will get you closer to what you want.

Let go of anger, and create cooperation

Anger is a powerful, often frightening emotion; it needn't be. You can bring it into, or out of, your life. You introduce anger into your life in several ways. One is when you react emotionally to your need to change things (your spouse's nagging, your secretary's dawdling, and your neighbors' barking dog). You get rapid relief from anger by staying out of the blame system (choosing to create the relationship you want, choosing to hold your secretary accountable by docking her pay, choosing to speak to your neighbors or to report them to the local animal control unit), thereby, not creating anger. We will look at some frequently asked questions about anger, and will help you learn how you can let go of it, or even better, never create it in the first place. I am devoting time to anger because it affects so many people, and because most people with anger problems end up being diagnosed bipolar (Manic Depressive). As I hope you will see, anger does not mean you are bipolar; it has mistakenly been associated with bipolar disorder.

"Can I get rid of anger right now?"

Yes, you can eliminate anger immediately by getting out of blaming. Anger is a product of blaming. If you don't blame, anger is not created. If anger is not created, you save a lot of energy related to the immediate, and distant, fallout related to getting angry.

There are other concepts that may be useful when looking at the anger reaction. I have never understood anger management. Anger management is accepting failure; to manage something you must have already created it. To manage a mess, you must have made a mess. To manage anger, you have to have already created it. That means you have created the problem. But, for the same reason I suggest not creating anger, it is useful to know how to avoid situations that may make creation of anger easier. Here are some ideas to help you understanding how to stay away from anger situations. "Use these three preemptive steps:

>   Identify potential, probable, or repetitive conflicts.
>   Remove, or stay away from, the conflict.
>   Create an alternative experience that you want.

Find the conflict

You can find conflict in every upsetting situation. Conflict can arise between what you want to happen and what you believe is keeping you from getting what you want. You can frequently identify conflict by the word <u>but</u> ("I want to sleep late, <u>but</u> the kids next door are making too much noise"). You can also have more than one conflict, or <u>but,</u> in a situation ("I want to have a good vacation <u>but</u> the car is broken down, I'm out of money, and all the kids are complaining").

<u>Remember the ACT' formula</u>:
>   Accept where you are.
>   Choose where you want to go.
>   Take action.

"Where does your anger come from?"

Anger is a complex response (generated in part from both the Central Nervous System –CNS- and the Autonomic Nervous System—ANS) coming from blaming. When you are faced with a perceived, or real, danger to your (or someone you have an attachment to) physical or psychological well-being, your ANS sends you signals to either fight, or to take flight. Anger is the CNS message sent by the brain after it has made a judgment that someone, or something, has created your unwanted experience. When you perceive a threat (CNS), whether real or imaginary, your heart beats faster, your adrenaline pumps (ANS), and your thoughts narrow to focus on the danger.

You may become angry at perceived psychological threats. You experience someone threatening your self-esteem, your reputation, your peace of mind, or your sense of well-being, and you explode in anger. Your ANS functions outside of your conscious control. When you perceive a danger (a coworker seems to have threatened you) you will get the signal from your ANS to fight or to withdraw. When you operate from the choice system you are able to eliminate anger when it arises for two reasons:

Because knowing that you are creating your own psychological experiences, you don't perceive others' treatment of you as a threat or danger to what you want to create. It is simply the removal of one choice. When there is no threat, there is no signal from your ANS. If you do create anger, you can relieve it immediately by accepting that you are creating it, choosing the experience you want, and taking action to get it. "I accept the fact that I'm creating anger, because of the way I perceived his behavior toward me." "I will choose to envision a good relationship with him." "I will take several slow breaths; I will think of some good times we had in the past; I will ask him to join me for a cup of coffee at break time so we can talk, and I will honestly tell him how I didn't like what he did."

"Why does my anger feel so good at times?"

Anger feels good for a number of reasons. When you believe others are responsible for your unhappiness, your anger feels right, and justified.

If events go your way, you call it "fair"; if they go against you, you call it "unfair." When you think something, or someone, has been unfair to you, your anger feels well deserved. All anger feels like righteous anger. You think an act to eliminate unfairness will set your world right, and it feels justified. Some people (authors included) feel anger plays a roll in motivating people to action, and it is, therefore, a good thing. My point of view is we need to learn to act, and whether we act should not have to be tied to, or motivated by, anger. I believe it is actually the intensity of our feelings, when we are angry, that frightens many people; the intensity of feelings prevents them from acting, more often than it helps to generate action.

Fairness is a mental concept, a psychological label, or judgment you put on events. The label comes from you, not from something outside. Judgments are often made very quickly, and they often have little to no supportive evidence once we assess the situation. I recall my first impression of my roommate to be when I went to college. I saw this guy, and I told myself I hope I don't have to room with him. He looked cocky, arrogant and insensitive. I don't recall having thoughts about anyone else in the room at the time. Guess what. He was assigned to be my roommate. He later became best man at my wedding. (We call to ourselves that which we say we want the least—and sometimes it is for our own good.)

The physical universe is neither fair, nor unfair. It simply is. And the same principles apply to everyone. Daily in my office, I tell people that the experiences they are having, is because of their belief systems, and it is not a reflection of their goodness or badness; their experiences are just a product of their belief system. When we put our hand on a hot burner, the pain experienced is not because Mother Nature is being a bitch; Mother Nature is encouraging us not to put our hand on the burner. I believe most of the unpleasant experiences we have are because of Natures desire for us not do the behaviors, and to not have the thinking, that creates them.

Anger may be a way of trying to get rid of the feeling of anxiety, but it fails because you then have to deal with the consequences generated (destroyed relations, jail for destruction of property, or murder).

Anger feels good because you feel powerful when you're angry. This power is an illusion, because when you're angry you're usually less effective in making appropriate choices. Anger is frequently a response to feeling powerless; anger can generate a false sense of power.

When you are angry you are acting out your contempt for others. By cutting off others (psychologically or physically), you feel superior and better—for a moment. Even though your anger feels good, the relief is likely temporary; you can't set reality right and you aren't moving toward what you want when you are consumed with anger. We need to accept current reality and look for choices in it. But anger blocks your ability to do that and usually alienates us from others.

"Don't I have a right to get angry?"

You continually have the choice to get angry if you want to. Right has nothing to do with it. Some people think they have no choice about being angry; they believe anger is caused by the event, because it appears to them there is no time for rational thought to occur between the event and the response. This is an inaccurate perception. What happens in our mind is similar to what happens on a snowy slope after kids have slid down the same spot multiple times. That response gets really fast. In other words, we condition our mind to act in certain ways. This is the same process the gunfighter, or the Emergency Room staff creates with repeated practice. How other people act is their responsibility. How you think, feel, and act is yours.

The question is legitimate: Does anger help or hinder me? Anger is usually an attempt to change other people. You can intimidate other people with anger, but if you try to change them, you will generally experience strong resistance. People may "do you wrong," but if you keep your eye on solving the problem and take action to do that, rather than trying to change people so that they will "do you right," you will have a richer and happier life.

"Won't anger get me what I want?"

Although anger may make you feel more powerful, it usually won't get you what you want in the long run. You can at times use anger to get what you want, in the short run, by intimidating others. However, anger is a failure force. Anger blurs your vision, misdirects your attention, depletes your psychic energy, breeds other painful emotions, and destroys cooperation.

Anger blurs your vision. When you are angry, you focus on the emotion rather than on the issue. Your prime motivation becomes getting revenge, and you forget about what you really ought to do. Because you don't focus solely on your issue, you don't see solutions as clearly.

Anger misdirects your attention. Instead of looking for choices that will get you what you want, you look for ways to get even. You ruminate about what made you angry, and what you're going to do about it. Because your attention is focused on these details, you overlook the details that will take you where you originally wanted to go. You get so mad at the driver who cut in front of you that you miss your turnoff. (Many accidents occur after people get angry.)

Anger depletes your psychic energy. At any one time you have a limited amount of psychological energy, or focus. You need psychological energy to create what you want to happen. Getting angry is like slamming the throttle of your car to the floor when you are in neutral —you make a lot of noise, burn up your energy, but you don't actually get anywhere.

Anger is a major energy burner. Afterward, when your energy (ability to focus clearly) is low, you are more prone to other psychological problems, such as apathy and depression. You slip down the emotional ladder to lower levels. The path of least resistance is to turn toward the negative.

Anger breeds other painful emotions. When you are angry, your emotional distress can include:

Hurt-"Why did he have to say that to me? I thought he liked my work."

Fear-"I want to ask her out, but she might say something that will set me off."

Frustration-"I could kill the people who manufacture junk like this. I'm so sick and tired of buying cars that turn out to be lemons."

Resentment-" I'd have been a success, if it weren't for her."

Surface or superficial communications-"I'm afraid, if I really say what I mean, she'll get angry at me and we'll have a fight."

Low self-esteem-"I'll do just what they want, so no one will yell at me, and they won't make me lose my temper."

Anger destroys the spirit of cooperation. If you are chronically angry, people will avoid you. No one wants to form a lasting collaboration with someone who is always angry. Problems with anger are a significant reason for relationships going bad, and a major reason many people are unsuccessful on their jobs and in their careers.

"Won't anger get other people to do what I want?"

Getting angry is a tactic to change others. Manipulations are when you say, or do something, you believe will cause an emotional reaction in others—make them feel good or bad—and thereby prompt them to act as you want. Needing to change others naturally leads to manipulation. If you think others prevent you from getting what you want, you feel you must emotionally maneuver them into doing what you want. Anger is a common manipulation tactic, because most people are easily manipulated by it ("If I don't have dinner ready at six every night, my husband gets upset").

Aggressive people use anger to manipulate others ("make" them scared), passive people use withdrawal to manipulate others ("make" others feel sorry or guilty). Withdrawal is an attempt to get just far enough away from others to make them feel responsible for you. Assuming a forlorn look, you ignite others' rescue fantasies ("I can't let him feel so bad").

Although homicide is less common than suicide, it is another, final act in holding others responsible for your life.

Many explanations have been given for the high rate of violence in America, but the possibility that murderers kill, because they blame others for their problems, is often overlooked. A man who killed twenty-one people in a fast-food restaurant was mad at the world. According to the Los Angeles Times, he "blamed such external forces as former President Jimmy Carter, the Trilateral Commission, high interest rates and the Federal Reserve Board for his career failures." If you look at any of the school shootings, they are all prompted by "blame." It is my unofficial belief that blame has killed more people than all of the diseases mankind has encountered. Listen to the rhetoric from the news reports coming out of the mid East.

People usually try to manipulate others when they feel powerless to change a situation directly. It's a last-ditch effort, because you don't know what else to do. Your anger is an attempt to gather strength to overcome your enemies. Anger is an admission that you lack other means for getting what you want. Power plays are lose/lose situations ("I'll make him marry me by getting pregnant"). You may think you'll be top seal on the warm rock, but both of you end up in cold water. Although you can isolate yourself to some degree from others, you still have to deal with people throughout your life. If you use cooperation, rather than power, to achieve your goals (and theirs), everyone wins.

"What if someone gets angry?"

If you cave in to avoid someone's anger, you are allowing yourself to be manipulated. You may even train other people on how to manipulate you, by telegraphing what makes you feel bad. If you're sensitive to rejection, they'll use withdrawal; if you're sensitive to threats, they will use anger.

You can avoid being manipulated by others by refusing to allow them to "make you" feel bad. Take accountability for your feelings, and recognize you are always responsible for your feelings. Refuse to assign your bad feelings to others ("He "<u>made me</u>" feel awful when he yelled at me"). Use the ACT to stay on target:

"I accept the reality that my boss is yelling at me."

"I choose to feel good about myself, and to enjoy my work."

"I will take action by asking the boss for specific ways I can be of benefit to the company, and by asking him to notify me as soon as I don't meet his requirements, rather than waiting until he gets angry."

Anger has a tendency to breed anger. By responding in kind, you put yourself in a weaker position. If you get angry at someone, that person is likely to become even more furious, and an argument can escalate into a war. If someone, who is trying to manipulate you, gets any emotional reaction out of you, you usually end up losing.

Take the initiative and set the emotional tone. If you have to deal with angry clients, customers, employees, or family members, your best bet is to see if you can improve the emotional tone of the interaction. Irritation, annoyance, and boredom are the emotional states above anger.

The best way to raise the emotional tone is to ask the angry person questions in a calm manner. A good question is, "Is there anything else bothering you?" After repeatedly stating what is making them angry, people generally lose steam; their anger turns to irritation, and they eventually get bored with what originally made them angry. At this point, they often become interested in solving the problem. Anger with the threat of violence is usually used to maintain a power position. Angry people often strike out, and they can physically hurt you (the stalker); their manipulation may become physical. They try to make you fear their anger. Others may also try to use power over you ("If you don't do what I want, you'll be sorry"), but you always have the choice not to go along with the demand. Accept your reality, and look within it for choices. Gather facts that can help you. Are there shelters for battered women near you? What are their phone numbers? If you call the police, how quickly will they arrive? Can you afford to move away from abusive neighbors? Would marriage counseling help resolve the continuous bickering between you and your spouse?

Don't be helpless. The area in which you feel the most powerless is often, precisely, the area where you have more ability than anyone else to get what you want.

You can choose to work toward what you want in life, and then create it. Make the choices that will take you there, even if you need to make such major choices as divorce, or relocation.

"Isn't anger at myself a good way to get motivated?"

Anger can be a strong motivator, but the costs are high. Using emotions to manipulate you has some serious drawbacks:

- You turn your life over to your feelings, instead of to your creative ability to choose what you want to happen. You let your feelings (the tail) "wag the dog."
- You have to keep the strong negative emotions at high intensity, lest you lose your motivation energy once the emotions drop.
- You make yourself more vulnerable to being manipulated by others,
- You undermine your self-esteem, waste your energy, and give your mind conflicting messages ("I'm a terrible person for doing that, but I'm also a good person who will never do it again").

Anger is unnecessary

You can set limits with others ("If you don't do your job, I'll let you go"; "If you go out with others, I will no longer go out with you") without having to get angry. You can be honest without having to use anger to override your inhibitions. You can motivate yourself with the vision of what you want to do, rather than with anger at what you didn't want to do.

"Isn't it a good idea to express anger to people who make us mad?"

Although a whole school of thought suggests that you are better off when you tell others off, a great deal of recent research has found the opposite to be the case. Social psychologists have been studying what is called "expressed emotionality"—this is where people "let it all hang out" and verbally express their hostility. In recent studies researchers have found that mental patients who return to homes with highly expressed emotionality are much more likely to have relapses than those who return to homes with low expressed emotionality. Recent research has also shown that this detrimental effect similarly affects depressed people and people trying to lose weight. When others try to nag the depressed person into being happy, or the obese person into losing weight, the problem generally gets worse, not better.

If you are in the position of having someone use anger, or some other expressed emotion to change you, be aware that you will have an inclination to do the opposite of what they want. You can end up in a no-win situation if it's a matter of problem behavior you're trying to deal with—either you do what they want and you lose, or you continue with the problem behavior and you lose. The way out is to do what's in your best interest in spite of what they are doing ("I'm going to lose weight even if you are nagging me to lose weight"; "I'm going to get up and get active despite the fact that you're angry at me for staying in bed").

Other researchers have found that freely venting your anger corrodes relationships and breeds more anger, not less. Psychologists Jeanette and Robert Laver studied what makes a happy marriage. Only one out of 300 happily married couples reported that they yell at each other.

The happy couples in the study emphasized the importance of restraint in expressing emotions. A salesman with a thirty-six-year happy marriage gave a typical response: "Discuss your problems in a normal voice. If a voice is raised, stop. Return after a short period of time. Start again. After a period of time both parties will be able to deal with their problems and not say things they will be sorry about later."

How can I prevent anger?

First of all, stay out of blaming!

There are five other constructive ways you can prevent anger in yourself:

> Let go of expectations.
> Be self-accountable.
> Make a decision.
> Be honest.
> Create cooperation.

Let go of expectations

Negative and positive expectations blind you to the real opportunities for happiness and achievement that exist in current reality. They undermine your vision. When you insist on a specific means to something ("Bill is the only one I could be happily married to"), you overlook your choices. If that particular "how" doesn't happen and you get angry, you blind yourself to the other "hows" that may get you what you want (other people with whom you could have a satisfying relationship). If what you want doesn't happen the way you expect it to, you believe that it will never happen.

Expectations are different from your visions. Expectations often lead to failure. Expectations usually revolve around one of your habitual side issues (worth, control, trust, perfection, belonging, achievement). You start to expect you'll get (or won't get) some psychological commodity you believe you need.

The way out of the expectation trap is to focus on the vision you want to create ("I want to feel good about myself at the party"), not on "how" or "if" it will happen. Expect the unexpected and focus on your vision. Separate your expectations, what you think should happen, from what you want to create.

For example, let go of the expectation that your vacation will be perfect (no car trouble, clean hotels, good weather), and hold the vision that you will find ways to enjoy yourself no matter what happens on your vacation. Let go of the expectation that everyone will laugh at you if you ask a stupid question in class, and hold the vision that you will seek and gain knowledge from the class. Let go of the expectation that someone will ask you out on Friday night, and hold the vision that you will enjoy yourself Friday night, whether you are asked out, or not. Life is full of surprises. The best overall stance is to expect nothing and get ready for everything.

Be self-accountable

You likely did something directly or indirectly to bring about the situation that triggers your anger. Maybe you failed to look at all the possibilities before you jumped into a project. Because you didn't look at the possibilities (the project could last a full year; the project could involve financial sacrifice; it could involve significant time away from home), you are caught off guard. You get angry at the project leader or at your coworkers, who don't seem to be pulling their share of the load, or at your family, who can't understand your absences. If you look objectively at the situation, you can see the role you played ("I didn't pay attention to all the ramifications of getting involved in the project").

When you hold yourself accountable, you can more clearly see what to do about the situation ("I can resign from the project"), and you can better assess the price you may have to pay (misunderstanding by coworkers, hard feelings on the part of the leader). If you are willing to pay the price (relocate, look for a new job, leave your marriage, refuse to give your daughter money if she doesn't get a job), you can always do something about your situation once you learn to recognize the role you played in causing it.

In the psychological world you can nearly always create the experience you want. In the physical world what looks like someone blocking your way is merely the removal of one choice. You may not see the choice you want, but that doesn't mean it's absent. Hold the tension between where you are and what you want, and your choices will appear.

For example, you might say, "I am stuck in this job, and I don't like it because the manager constantly checks on me; I accept this situation, and I hold the vision of what I want—to be in an interesting job where I am trusted." Any number of choices may appear: speaking with the manager about how to gain his or her trust, going to night school to broaden your skills, speaking with a coworker about whether or not you provide reason to be mistrusted, or using vacation days to apply for other jobs.

Or, you might say, "I accept the fact that right now my marriage isn't sexually satisfying, and sex is important to me. I hold the vision of a warm physical relationship with my husband." Choices will appear according to your situation: having an honest talk with your husband, going to marriage counseling, consulting sex manuals for ways to spice up your side of it, confiding in a doctor. You may find that you need to adjust your vision to "having a warm physical relationship with someone." If your husband is totally unresponsive to your requests to work the situation out, or to your physical advances, then your choices may involve separation, divorce, and finding ways to meet new people.

Make a decision

Anger may appear to come from an unwillingness to make a decision, usually because you try to avoid being accountable for your actions. When you're angry about something, you usually don't like the alternatives. You have choices, but because you dislike them, you pretend that you don't have any at all. You don't have to act in some way to get your anger to go away. Merely deciding on a course of action usually dispels the anger.

Let go of loneliness and create Intimacy

Loneliness is a common painful experience. All of us feel it at one time or another. You feel lonely when you fail to connect with others on a psychological level. Even if your physical world coexists with another's, your psychological worlds are frequently separate and disjointed. Alone, or with other people, you may feel lonely, isolated, and vulnerable. When you're experiencing loneliness, you feel separated and cut off from others.

One of the contributors to this state is that your acceptor is blocked—you're not accepting yourself, or others; you're not in the flow.

Another contributor to loneliness is our failure to understand we are a part of a larger whole. Anwar Suddat described his evolving realization of this while he was a political prisoner, kept in isolation for years.

Intimacy is one of the concepts that have both a mental and physical attribute. We can be psychologically intimate with someone we have just met, or with someone we have not seen for years. We can lack physical intimacy with the husband, or wife, we live with, or we can be forced through rape to the extreme of sexual intimacy by someone we loath. Desired intimacy (physical or emotional) is one of the cures for loneliness. Intimacy flows two ways. If you accept other people for whom they are, despite what they say, and what they do, hopefully, they will do the same for you. You are more natural, and more yourself when you feel as if the other person accepts you. You have more confidence to speak, or to act, because you don't assume you'll be rejected. This is the base of the origin of many affairs. A man, or woman, gets into a conversation with a stranger. Since they do not know the person, they have no need to be dishonest with them (ie: they do not need to protect the other person's feelings), and in a few minutes they may actually share more intimate moments than they have with their spouse over a number of years. It feels good, so the decision is made to do it again.

When you feel intimate with others, you are allowing yourself to know and be known. Knowing is how you connect with others, and with the world. Poet and philosopher Eli Siegel said that we get to know, and like, the world, and ourselves, on an honest basis by getting to know another person.

You develop intimacy by seeing how others are the same, or different from you. People bothered by loneliness often say, "other people are just like me, so why bother?" or "We have nothing in common, so why bother?" Intimacy is getting to know how you are similar and different from others. Intimacy is accurate non-defensive communication with others. Intimacy is allowing other people into our space emotionally and physically: sometimes in only one way and at the exclusion of the other. Young girls, or boys, bent on an intimate relationship may have sex with a partner to try and dull the sense of not being loved, or, of not being a part of a larger whole. Rather than trying to know others, so you can define them, you get to know them sexually with the hope you can accept them, accept yourself, and accept the world later.

Loneliness is contributed to by confusion over your degree of responsibility. You are only responsible for what you can think, feel, and do. You don't have the ability to respond for others (make them call you for a date), and they don't have the ability to respond for you (make you get out of the house, and get involved with other people). If you are lonely the likelihood is that you are trying to defend yourself from some perceived hurt or pain. In the blame world the three ways people attempt to protect themselves are to put up walls, create distance in the relationship, and to turn off feelings. We may also attempt to control the situation by trying to change others (get them to ask you out, get them to involve you in activities), or hoping we can change (get up the nerve to go to the club meeting).

To create intimacy, you first have to communicate honestly with others. You want to stop creating loneliness. In other words, stop holding others accountable for your experiences and for trying to change them; it only leads to frustration and generates more of a sense of vulnerability and failure.

When you think you have to change others or the world to achieve intimacy, your communication is (1) shallow, because you are afraid to say what you mean, or to hear what the other person means, and (2) manipulative, because you choose words and actions intended to change others, or intended to try and keep them from being upset with you. Surface communication and manipulative communication create a sense of isolation and loneliness. The following categories of communication will help you catch yourself when you start to move into the blame system.

Surface communication

Selective, secretive communication, blame and fear of blame strangle a relationship. You may be so used to not saying what you really mean that you don't say anything even if it's pleasant. The other person cannot read your mind, and they may interpret your thoughts with total inaccuracy.

WIFE: "What are you thinking?"

HUSBAND: "Oh, nothing." (Thinking: "Where would be a nice place to take her tonight?")

WIFE (snaps): "I know better." (Thinking: "He is thinking about wanting to be with his friends and has forgotten all about saying we would go out tonight.")

HUSBAND: "No, really." (Thinking: "The hell with her, I'll go out with my friends.")

WIFE: "You're impossible."

HUSBAND: "You're always complaining." (Thinking: "Why is she attacking me? I don't deserve it.")

WIFE: "Well, if you would talk to me once in a while, it wouldn't be so boring around here."

HUSBAND (getting angry): "So you think it's boring here, do you? Well, why don't you go back and live with your mother, if you want to be around someone really exciting?"

WIFE (feeling rejected): "You're always trying to get rid of me! You don't care about me at all."

HUSBAND (in reaction): "Well, if you don't think I care, why don't you get out?"

WIFE (angrily): "Well, maybe I will do just that." (She storms out.)

You train the other person to keep conversations superficial by reacting emotionally with anger, tears, or withdrawal. The only topic you can discuss without a fight is the weather.

Certain areas of life carry the taboo marker and there is an encouragement for deception; deception feeds back into the negative emotionality of the situation. You refrain from saying something because the topic causes the other person to get angry; then they get angry because you didn't say anything—and so it goes. But you don't talk about your deteriorating relationship, so the relationship continues to go down hill.

Once direct communication goes, you have to rely on manipulation, anger, silence, or withdrawal to get your point across. The relationship deteriorates even further, and you back away psychologically from each other. A wall goes up.

Lying

Dishonesty by omission (withholding the truth) or commission (telling an untruth) is a byproduct of the blame system. You don't tell the truth because you want to control the outcome. Adrienne Rich, in her book *On Lies, Secrets and Silence*, says, "Every liar lives in fear of losing control. She cannot even desire a relationship without manipulation, since to be vulnerable to another person means for her the loss of control. The liar has many friends, and leads an existence of great loneliness."

If others' displeasure can make you feel bad, you feel that you have to tell them what they want to hear. Lying becomes the only option for "making" others feel good. When you fail to tell the truth, minor issues escalate into major ones.

You reserve honesty as a last-ditch defensive weapon. You use it to hurt others, and you use it to get the upper hand ("Someone like you who would cheat on his business partner has no business trying to talk me into investing"). The solution is to always say what you want, and to let the chips fall where they will.

Fast talk-being a con artist

If you are highly verbal, you can use fast talk to manipulate others.

WIFE: "I want you to help out more with the yard work."

HUSBAND: "I want to help you, but we both know you lack self-esteem. And the only way you'll ever get any respect for yourself is by taking on and carrying out duties. If I were to start doing more of your jobs, I would be robbing you of your chance to develop self-esteem. I love you too much to let that happen."

Tuning out

When you are scared to rock the boat or to make waves ("One false move and I'll tip over and drown"), you avoid making waves at all, and you become watchful of what you say. Your messages become weak, complex, and peripheral.

You tune others out because it's the only way you believe you can get them to change. By refusing to listen to the other person, you force your way on them. If that maneuver fails, you withdraw until you get your way.

Explosive words

Tuning out is a natural defense against the belief that words can hurt you. If you think they can hurt you, you think they can hurt others, so you use words hurtfully ("You're just like your mother"). Explosive words lead to big blowups.

Arguments

Arguments are staples in the blame system. You take the offensive to change others and the defensive to resist being changed. If you are afraid of getting close to others, this is a way to stay connected, but distant at the same time. Rather than accepting differences, you try to mold others into your image.

Side effects of isolation communication

Loss of Spontaneity When communication breaks down, spontaneity goes. You begin to rehearse what you're going to say ("If he says _____ I'll say _____"; "When she says 'good morning,' I'm going to say_____"), and you become over concerned with saying things perfectly, so that you can make an impression, get revenge, or appear brilliant. Being obsessed with what you are going to say hinders communication, because you stop listening and responding to what you hear. You speak from a script that you've written in advance.

Affairs

The probability of extramarital affairs increases as communication in the marriage decreases. People usually have affairs to avoid the painful interactions in their marriage and to get in touch with something that they feel is missing in their marriage.

At the beginning of an affair, you do not feel responsible for the other's feelings, so you're not trying to change the person. You feel free to be yourself and can spontaneously express what you're thinking, and what you're feeling. You have no strings attached. Your honesty feels great, but it's usually short-lived. Most often, you start taking responsibility for the other person's feelings, and once you do that, you're back in the hurt/loneliness cycle.

How do you communicate?

Loneliness, or emotional isolation, is the natural result of distancing from others. It is a protective mechanism: Distancing represents a logical step in the unrewarding blame system. You create what you expect ("Others hurt me, so I have to move away"). If others are responsible for your pain, you have to attack them, or you have to distance yourself from them.

How to develop laser communication

Communication should be a way of connecting; it is a way to develop intimacy. It is the bridge (of words, gestures, facial expressions, touch) by which you reach another person. When you use choice to create what you want, you communicate with synchronization, purity, and directness; like the laser. Laser communication is:

> Honest—how you communicate
> Timely—where and when you communicate
> Accurate—what you communicate
> Unifying—why you communicate
> Use the following steps to develop laser communication.

How to achieve honesty

Be specific. Stay at the concrete level ("When you borrow my sweater, please have it cleaned before you bring it back"), and avoid the abstract ("These situations always turn out like this"). Stick to the present ("This is how I feel right now"); avoid dragging up the abstract past or future ("You've never treated me right from the day we met").

Be direct

Say what you mean, and mean what you say ("I love you, and I want to make the relationship work"). Hinting, or expecting the other person to play Twenty Questions with you, diffuses and confuses what you want to say. The more direct you are the better.

Ask for what you want. Free yourself of your bias against asking for what you want. People are not mind readers, and if you expect the other person to guess what you want, very likely you won't get it.

Be straight

Make your thoughts, feelings, and actions move in the same direction. Get rid of double messages ("I'm not questioning your decision; I just want to know why you made it"). Be aware that ambivalence ("I want to do it, and I also don't want to do it.") is an attempt to avoid accountability.

Be clear

First think about what you want to tell the other person, then tell them in the straightest and simplest way you can ("I would like to have this job"). Although too much planning can hamper communication (as when you rehearse what you are going to say); some planning can help you. Too much planning is attempting to control how the conversation will go despite what the other person may or may not, say. "Just enough planning" is having your facts (current reality), and knowing the ideas you want to get across (your vision). It also involves taking the other person into account (for example, considering if your boss is more open to discussion before, or after, lunch). You usually have to create and adjust the conversation to get the result you want.

Create a climate for honesty

Encourage honesty in the other person. Instead of casting your eyes heavenward and muttering under your breath when someone says something you dislike, reinforce the person for being open ("I don't like hearing it, but I'm glad you brought it up").

Tell the truth early

Even if the other person becomes angry, tell the truth. Refuse to let the other person's attempt at manipulation, or denials, to take away your choice to be honest. Don't lie, even if you think it's going to get you what you want. It won't in the long run.

Tell the appropriate truth

To see whether, or not, the truth is appropriate in a situation, ask yourself three questions. (1) Does the person need to know the truth (Use common sense)? (2) Am I giving them a fair representation of the whole truth? (3)

Can I tell the truth in a kind way? If the answer is yes to any of the three questions, then tell the truth.

Timeliness: When to raise the issue, and when not to

Be sensitive to time and place. If you need to resolve a matter of any complexity, be aware that it will take at least an hour. Don't try to resolve a conflict as you walk up the porch steps to a dinner party. If your partner has only ten minutes to catch a plane, wait until a more appropriate time to bring up a complex issue.

Communicate to the other person when you are ready to move on. If you just want to get back at someone, wait. Many times the mere passage of time aids resolution.

Stick to one topic

Topic jumping diffuses energy and confuses the issues. Be aware of what you are talking about and stick to it ("Okay, we can deal with that in a moment, but let's finish this first").

Be accurate

Clarify. If you are unsure of what is being said, ask for clarification ("Please elaborate on what you mean by that"). Avoid inference, assumptions, and jumping to conclusions ("I'm not really sure what he said, but he must have been criticizing my work because that's the kind of boss he is"). Develop a mental picture of what the other person is saying. If the picture is fuzzy or unclear, ask the person to clarify it.

Go to the source

If you hear a rumor or remark that affects you, check it out with the primary person ("I heard you have a problem with my work. Is this true?"). Secondary sources have only secondary reliability.

Avoid the words always and never. They are red flag words, and they are rarely accurate: "You never do the dishes!" "Yes, I do. I did them last week." Already the discussion is off center. A more accurate statement is: "I'd like to discuss the housework and tell you what I would like to see happen."

Speak from the first person

Because you can only think, feel, and act for yourself, speaking from the first person is more accurate than from the second person. "You ignore me" may seem accurate to you, but to your partner it may not be, because he thinks he is just reading the newspaper. A more accurate statement would be, "I would like you to talk with me when I get home from work, rather than read the paper. What can we do about it?"

Err on the side of inclusion

Decide to include information, even if you don't believe it is needed, rather than to exclude it for fear of appearing foolish. If you're unsure about what is being said, say so. If you're not sure the other person understands you, repeat what you said. It is far better to appear foolish than to miss important information ("I know this is the third time I've asked, but I still don't understand what you're saying").

How to achieve unification

Listen. Tune in to what the other person is saying even if what you hear is painful. When you connect through listening, you create a climate in which the other person can be more honest, accurate, and timely with you. When you really listen, you can look within the relationship for what you need to improve the relationship.

Keep in touch

Absence does not always make the heart grow fonder. Look directly at the other person; use touch if you can. If the other person is at some distance, use frequent phone calls and letters to keep the bond between you strong.

Collaborate

Avoid secrets, or hidden, agendas. Refuse to keep information from someone to whom you're close. Collaborate ("How can we handle your mother's drinking?") with others; don't sabotage them ("He wants me to be nice to his mother, but if she takes a drink I'm going to be cold to her").

Be creative

Brainstorm ways to communicate. If you have trouble talking to someone in the morning, leave notes. Switch roles in order to understand the other side. Try solving a problem nonverbally. Draw pictures of how you feel, then draw pictures of what you would like to see happen. Play music with lyrics that express what you want. Play a game of charades, acting out what you feel, what you think the other person feels, what you want, how you could solve the problem together. Do an "interruptive dance" together, and try to reach a resolution by the end of the dance.

Let others be right

You can eliminate more than half of your communication difficulties by telling the other person "You may be right." You are verbally affirming their right to their own choices, the right to see the world as they see fit (which is theirs anyway). You aren't caving in, because you still have the right to your choices and the way you see the world ("You are right, but this is how I see it"; "You are right, but this is how I am going to do it"). Letting the other person be right sets the stage for cooperation.

Use after-action talk

Talk about how you communicated after a heated discussion ("We both seemed to get defensive about the custody issue, didn't we?"). "Did my comparing you to your brother help you, or make you angry?" "I felt defensive when you kept answering my questions with a question"). Get feedback from the other person. Welcome it, and learn from it. After-action talks can normalize confrontations and iron out communication problems.

Give concrete feedback

Use no-fault criticism. Ask if the person wants your input. If they say yes, stick to the facts on a concrete level without blaming ("I've noticed that when you are with your mother, you ... ").

Choose to accept criticism openly from others. Listen and be aware of how you can gain from others' feedback. No matter how unfair, exaggerated, and manipulative someone's remarks might be to you, you can nearly always learn something from it. When your feelings are hurt, you often have a chance to accept some useful truth about yourself. If you operate from the choice system, you can ask yourself. "What is true here?" Others may want to throw blame at you, but you can always find some helpful information from the feedback. Let go of the past; let go of past hurts, so that you can start anew.

Become aware of the feelings about past "buts" that might be clouding a present issue. Decide to act concretely, in the present, to create a common future, "What do we both want in the future?" What is our shared vision and common ground?" "I felt hurt when he was unfaithful to me, and I guess I'm transferring that to you; I'd like to accept that, and I would like to start fresh from right now," "I've learned a lesson from her gossip, but I don't need to make my day miserable by harping on it, because I do have to continue working with her. I'll be pleasant to her, but I'll be careful not to confide my private life to her anymore."

How to create good relationships

Honesty sets the stage for a healthy relationship. Whoever you are, when you are truly yourself, you are more confident and more attractive. When you choose to create your own life, you become yourself.

Imagine you are at a party and introduce yourself by saying, "Hi, I'm extremely dependent. I'm looking for someone to make me happy, and someone to shore me up emotionally." What do you imagine would happen? Now ask yourself how you might be saying this nonverbally (not listening, keeping to yourself, not looking someone in the eye, sighing).

Look at the situation objectively and decide if people would be attracted to you.

Except for rescuers, most people would move away from you. Social psychologists have found that people like emotionally independent people, and they dislike overly dependent people. The more self-confident and emotionally self-reliant you are, the more people will be attracted to you.

Look at the film stars who attract a solid following. Katharine Hepburn, Robert Redford, Paul Newman, Clint Eastwood. Each has an image of emotional self-reliance. Researchers at the University of Utah found that marriages based on healthy dependency, as opposed to unhealthy dependence, lasted longer, and they were of higher quality.

The issue is not dependency versus independency, but is more about change versus choice. Change dependence is based on a need for others to make you happy. This tends to drive others away, and you end up lonelier than ever. Change independence is a need to move away from others, because you believe they can hurt, or control you. Your independence (self-absorption) and compulsive self-reliance are strategies to protect yourself—you're afraid others will take over if you invite them to help you. My patients often make the mistake of thinking that the opposite of dependency is independency. This misconception leads to isolation and more loneliness. The opposite of dependency is actually healthy dependency. Learning to depend on others in a healthy way fosters a sense of trust and mutual caring.

To create anything of note and to be able to form a relationship with others, you need healthy dependence. When you convey self-accountability for your own feelings, others feel comfortable with you, and they are willing to cooperate more with you. They move toward you. A healthy independence is simply your awareness that you create your own experiences in the areas that you should. You are the author of your own life, and you don't need others to plot it out for you.

To create a relationship, you can use the principles of acceptance, vision, and choice. You tap into your intuition for the type of relationship you want. You hold that vision, and then you make the choice to have it, and you follow your hunches to make it happen. Once you start to meet people, you need to focus on knowing them.

How to build to intimacy

Use the following techniques to enhance the type of knowing that leads to intimacy. Decide to know the other people in your life instead of taking them for granted. When you meet other people, or you go on dates, rather than trying to impress, or possess them, ask yourself how you could get to know them better; make that your aim. When you want to get to know people, listen to them. They, in turn, will usually want to know more about you. They will begin to listen to you, and true communication will be established.

Interview people and become a focused listener. You can practice on strangers you meet or on people you see every day. Interview others with goodwill; use what they say as a way to get to know them, not as a way to put them down. "You seem to enjoy meeting the people who come through your line. How long have you been a cashier?" "You seem tired today. Did you have a hard day?" "That's a lovely sweater. Are you interested in knitting?" "I saw your wife at the store with your grandson. Is he with you for the summer?"

Let go of your need to possess, or own, the other person. See how getting to know the other person can help you connect with others, rather than using the other person to help you put up a wall between you and the world ("It's us against the world").

Consider how you can earn others' goodwill. Rather than looking to see how others are taking advantage of you; ask yourself what you can do for them.

Accept your insecurity with others. In all relationships there is a degree of insecurity ("Will they like me? Will I continue to like them?"). You have to be willing to accept this insecurity to get to know the person more completely.

See knowing as a process. Rather than having to know a person all at once, let the relationship develop naturally on all levels.

> Shame-"I'll feel terrible, if I don't do this for you."
> Resentment-"You made me love you."
> Desperation "What can I do to make you love me?"
> Low self-esteem-"You have to do this for me to prove that you love me."
> Fear-"You'll be angry with me, if I don't give this to you."
> Bitterness-"I get nothing back from my investment in the relationship."

Live in the Choice System

When you love, you choose to accept others as they are. You appreciate the ways in which they are the same as you and yet different. You connect with the sameness, and appreciate the differences. You get immediate enjoyment from the love you give, and that you receive. If you give love, no one owes you, and if you receive love, you do not owe anyone.

Love by choice is mature, sustaining, and transcends infatuation and physical attractions. Because it comes from within you, love can be fostered and expanded. This is a love you can create; you don't have to fall into it. Use the steps in the ACT Formula:

> Accept the other person.
> Choose love.
> Take action to bring that love about.

Acceptance is a large part of loving others. Accept them as they are at the moment, and accept the idea that they have the responsibility for their own experiences.

Researchers have found that good marriages result from a combination of commitment and friendship. The crucial success force in a good relationship is commitment: valuing the vision of love enough to make it happen. If you devalue the other person, or the relationship, you kill the commitment. If you make the choice to value yourself, the other person, and the relationship, you have committed to the vision. That commitment sets the creation of love in motion. You are already more than halfway there. When you choose to love someone, or something, you will automatically start to move up the emotional scale. Think about what you can choose to love about something you're resisting. An attitude of love will help you move closer to your vision. When you give love, you will automatically get it back.

To go the rest of the way to your vision, act as if you do love the person. This is one of the most important principles in the psychological world: You can create feelings by your actions. If you want to care for your car, your dog, your child, your wife, or your husband, then take care of them. You care about what you take care of. To be interested, act interested. To be enthusiastic, act enthusiastic. To create love, treat the other person in a loving way. Here are some "action" suggestions to get you started:

> Put your partner's welfare before your own. For example, learn to stop what you are doing when your partner asks you something. Instead of saying, "Wait a minute," do what he or she asks you to do.

> Go out for your partner's favorite food instead of insisting on having your own way when selecting a restaurant.

> See your partner's favorite movie.
> Be gracious with your partner's friends.
> Let go of your partner's weaknesses, rather than holding onto them.
> Model the behavior you prefer.
> Be neither teacher, nor therapist.
> Ask if your partner wants your feedback; ask at the right time.

> Give your partner time ("I'll be glad to talk about this, whenever you're ready").

> Ask yourself how you can increase your partner's range of choices ("You can come with me or not; either one is fine with me").

> If your partner closes down your options, increase your own alternatives, rather than closing down your partner's options.

Seek to reconcile your differences. Attempt to see your partner's point of view, and then see how you both can win. Seek to reconcile differences as quickly as possible. You can rapidly resolve arguments by using the ACT Formula. Ask yourself what you can do to improve the relationship through direct or indirect ways. Sit down with a spirit of love, and calmly seek a common vision; accept your differences, choose a shared vision, and work out the details.

See the truth in your partner's truth.

Let your partner have their truth ("You're right from your point of view").

Use your notebook to keep a journal of all the ways you subtract from the relationship: greed, fear, anger, impatience, immaturity, lack of sincerity, demands, willfulness, putting yourself first, complaining to others, intolerance, discouragement, ignoring, taking for granted, jealousy, put-downs (for example, reading a book or watching the ball game on TV while at the dinner table), comparing to others.

Observe yourself without judgment. Objectively ask yourself how you might cause the other person trouble.

Be honest and assertive. Be open about what you think, feel, and do. Emphasize self-honesty, not your partner's flaws ("I'm feeling ignored" rather than "You're ignoring me"). An honest blame is just about as bad as a dishonest blame.

Appreciate your partner. Tell your partner what you like about him, or her, as often as possible.

Place emphasis on the small things ("I appreciate your putting gas in the car"). Be affectionate, especially when your partner is feeling down.

Show affection and appreciation even when your partner is in a bad mood.

Be affectionate in word and deed.

Do something for your partner at every opportunity: Bring a gift; give a loving word.

Do some secret service for your partner. This is one of the most important suggestions of all for creating loving feelings via your actions. Do one of the other person's usual jobs (feed the dog, fill the car with gas, put his or her clothes away).

Solve a problem for your partner without the person asking you to: replace a light bulb, fix a broken door, return some unwanted merchandise. Try to do one secret service each day. Doing good things for others is love in action. You can create love by doing well. John Wesley, the eighteenth-century clergyman, captured this idea in a poem:

> Do all the good you can.
> In all the ways you can
> In all the places you can
> At all the times you can
> To all the people you can
> As long as ever you can.

A good relationship has a certain easiness to it. When you are out of the blame system, you don't have to work at intimacy (connecting with another's psychological world). It is there for you naturally when you choose to let go of fear and when you create connections between you and others.

Let go of depression and create good self-esteem

If you are depressed, you may feel that you're incapable of getting out of the depressed state. You may not believe that accepting yourself is possible. You may feel that you can't even get out of bed. Depression can be a frightening emotion, because you feel so cut off from the world, as if a layer of cotton surrounds you. The feeling of depression can seem overwhelming, but remember it may be just a feeling (something you can affect by how you think and act).

Why do we feel depression?

When you are happy, you focus on gain and ignore loss ("It's true I don't want to be transferred, but I'll be closer to the mountains, and I can ski more often"). The reverse is true when you are depressed: You focus on loss and ignore gains ("If I'm transferred, I'll lose the best view in the building"). When you are depressed, you focus on the negative, and you create sadness. Sadness is nature's way of motivating you to make different choices, so you can get on with your life.

Depression is usually preceded by a series of events: hurt, dissatisfaction, disapproval, helplessness ("I can't change reality"), hopelessness ("Nothing will change it"), demoralization and finally depression.

Demoralization and depression can be malignant end products of the blame system of thinking. It is the final resignation, something is a particular way, and there is no hope that it will change. Because you need it to change, and it doesn't, giving up seems the only alternative.

You see yourself as a loser after repeated failure at trying to change others, yourself, or the world. You lose respect for yourself, and you become depressed. Your need for reality to be different creates psychological dissidence and, frequently, even the pain of depression. When you carefully separate out what you can do something about (your own thoughts, feelings and actions), from what only others can do something about (their own thoughts feelings and actions), you increase your immediate success from about 6% to 85%.

Depression runs in the same crowd with low self-esteem and poor self-respect. Once you regain your self-esteem, you are no longer on the road to feeling less, or no, depression.

Rating your self-esteem

Most people have trouble with self-esteem, because they tie it to some external event. To make yourself depressed, all you have to do is raise the requirements for feeling good about yourself. Keep upping the ante until self-esteem is out of reach. You might think, "I make $25,000 a year, but I need $40,000 to be happy. Then, if you do make $40,000, you say, "I need $60,000." Your desire to change things comes from cementing your self-esteem to some requirement or need. You believe you need more love, more money, more success, or more status to gain your own respect. The solution is to uncouple your psychological world of self-esteem from your stature in the physical world.

Depressed? Get active to get relief

Paradoxically, one way to separate you from the physical world is to get more active in it. Depression is often maintained by over thinking and under acting—you have difficulty focusing on anything but the negative. When you approach the physical world (get more active), you feel more connected to the world. Your focus shifts away from your negative view of yourself and toward what you want to create. Your action activates positive memories and disproves the negative thoughts that you can't do anything. Depression is at the bottom of the emotional scale; as you get more involved in the physical reality, your emotional tone can only go up.

Depression can result from trying to escape from reality. Attempts to escape reality are generally by-products of the blame system. You become self-absorbed in your thoughts and feelings. Getting active counteracts your attempts to escape. It enables you to accept and to assimilate current reality.

The first step in letting go of your depression is to accept the fact that you are depressed, and then to do what needs to be done anyway. Create more purposeful activity in your life; schedule your day. When you become depressed, your normal range of activities is disrupted. Establishing a schedule and then working the schedule may help get out of the depression.

You can benefit from planning your daily activities in detail. It is one way to create the life you want. The schedule gives you a sense of direction and mastery, as you focus on planned activities. Don't undertake an activity just for the sake of activity. Have some result, or destination, in mind before you start the activity. Walk to the beach to see the sunset, not just to be walking.

Guidelines for a daily anti-depression schedule

Schedule one day at a time. Do one task at a time. Don't worry about future tasks. If you finish one task early, engage in a pleasurable activity between tasks, such as reading, or taking a walk. The idea is to engage in activities, not to perform them perfectly. The benefit comes from the actual doing.

Plan with flexibility

If an unexpected event occurs, you may switch your plans. For example, if a friend unexpectedly calls, adjust your schedule accordingly. Activities that absorb your interest and concentration are best: cooking meals, cleaning the house, taking walks, filing, making phone calls, writing letters and memos. If the task seems too complicated, break it down into smaller steps ("Finish the annual report: (1) get out paper, pencils, and calculator; (2) complete statistical work; (3) finish introduction; (4) finish next two sections; (5) finish conclusion"). If the task seems too overwhelming, go to more simple tasks. No step is too small. You may feel too overwhelmed even to begin the annual report. If so, write a letter, clean your desk, make the coffee, or do some filing. Cleaning the clutter on your desk may be the first step to cleaning the clutter in your mind.

Your activity schedule should be related to your normal activities: getting up in the morning, making breakfast, exercising, taking a walk, talking with someone, answering mail, checking the answering machine, punching your time card. The planned activity should not be too specific, or too general. Shoot for something in between ("I'll read the paper for thirty minutes" instead of "I'll do some reading"). The last activity you schedule for the day should be sitting down to schedule the next day's activities. Developing activity schedules may take some time; you may have to spend thirty minutes to schedule just one day.

Choose ten daily depression fighters

Another good strategy for letting go of depression is to choose ten activities that you want to accomplish every day. With this strategy you don't have to construct a schedule for each day. Look for activities you would like to do each day. For example, one depressed person selected the following ten activities that she wanted to accomplish daily, and listed them in her notebook where she could refer to them daily:

> Get out of bed by 8:30 each morning.
> Prepare breakfast.
> Talk with someone in person, or by phone.
> Walk the dog.
> Read the newspaper.
> Do some yardwork.
> Make a good dinner.
> Do something with my son.
> Ride my exercise bike for ten minutes.
> Go to bed.

Another person selected these ten activities:

> Get out of bed by 7:00 A.M.
> Ride exercise bike for fifteen minutes.
> Prepare breakfast,
> Get to work by 8:55
> Complete phone calls.
> Walk for fifteen minutes during lunch.
> Keep filing current.
> Finish correspondence.
> Watch something I like on TV.
> Read.

When you do these activities, do them in a way that allows you to merge and connect with your physical reality. Stay focused on the task at hand, not on the next task. Stay focused until that specific task is accomplished.

Choose to do it

You always have the choice to act in some way. You may feel you can't get out of bed, but you can always hang your feet over the bed and dangle them.

Pay attention

When you get out of bed, get out of bed. Focus on which foot hits the floor first.

Do it with style.

See if you can make an art form out of getting up as quickly as you can. Put devotion into it. Make the activity the sole purpose of your life. Get out of bed, as if it were what you were born to do.

Accept your feelings

David Reynolds, in his book *Playing All on Running Water*, suggests that you accept your depression, and that you do what is necessary (get out of bed) to get what you want (feeling good again). Don't be at the mercy of your feelings ("I can't get out of bed, because I'm depressed, and I'm depressed, because I don't get out of bed"). When you're trying to change your depression, you blame your depression for your lack of action, and you blame yourself for being depressed. Rather than try to change your depression, accept it; choose to do an activity, and then do it. In some circles this is known as "Picking one's self up by the boot straps."

Get interested

As you do your daily activities, look for what is interesting in them. Once you are interested in the world (focus on it), you will come to know it;

once you know the world, you can like it; once you like it, you will like yourself better.

Switch topics

You can get immediate relief by focusing on the world instead of yourself. One of your response abilities is to put your focus outside of you, even if only for a second. If you are ruminating about yourself, switch to a new topic: what your child did in school, what the news anchor is saying, how the sky looks.

Accepting losses

When you are depressed, you often have some major losses you need to accept. If you have not clearly defined the loss, your depression may seem overwhelming ("I'm a loser") rather than specific ("I've lost my job"). A helpful strategy is to label, or name, what you need to accept. Ask yourself what it is you have lost, and try to answer specifically ("my reputation," "my promotion," "my sense of worth," instead of "everything," "all hope of happiness," "all chance of ever getting married"). Labeling allows you to specify the loss, so that you can deal with it. Once you put a name on it, you'll find it easier to digest.

Another obstacle may be that the type of label you put on the loss, or setback, prevents acceptance. You add symbolic meaning by incorrect labeling, and that surplus meaning makes the loss too big to accept. You can try re-labeling, or, even better, do not label at all. When we label, we carry the label with us from one moment to another. By not labeling, we enable our mind to focus on the moment, let go of the moment, and then we can move on.

You create your own psychological experiences by the way you label your current reality, whether you are talking about the weather or life in general. If you label reality negatively, you generate misery. It is useful to be aware that in life, labeling leads to carrying things around with you. A person who does not label is immersed in the event. This immersion leads to an experience, but not to a label. When a label is attached, we then carry the experience with us indefinitely.

People in power often re-label reality for those under them. An employee says, "We have a problem with the Smith account," and the manager re-labels it: "No, it's not a problem; this is what we'll do." Many problems in life are solved by someone in power re-labeling them ("Your son isn't a delinquent; he's just developing healthy independence"). Government does a lot of re-labeling, too; an "unacceptable" level of unemployment, or rate of inflation, becomes acceptable with the change of administration. Each administration labels reality to serve its interest. You can buy the labels others give, or make up your own; that's your choice.

Life and labels: the three umpires

In life, events are only events until you label them. You step out of your door and someone says "Nice day" to you. That event is neither good, nor bad, until you label it ("Nice of him to say that" versus "I hate it when people say that"). You experience the event according to the label you place on it.

Consider the story of the three umpires discussing how they call balls and strikes. The first says, "I call them as I see them." The second says, "I call them as they are." The third says, "They aren't anything until I call them."

Call your own game

Whether you realize it, or not, you do call your own game. How you call your game depends on what kind of an umpire you are.

> First Umpire Characteristics: You realize that events might differ from the way you see them, but in general, you rely on your perceptions. You see what you believe, and you believe what you see. You alter your perception if the evidence is strong enough; you don't see your beliefs as chiseled into concrete.

Second Umpire Characteristics: You are zealous about your opinions. No argument is sufficient; no proof is adequate to budge you from your position. You are frequently in error, but never in doubt (at least never outwardly). You talk at others, and you give them little opportunity to talk with you; your conversations generally turn into indoctrination seminars, or brainwashing ceremonies. You use indignation to put others "in their proper place," You know what is right for everybody.

The second umpire has many faces: the religious zealot, the censor, the revenger, the know-it-all, and paternalistic government. A major second umpire characteristic is that you do not think; on any issue your motto is, "I don't think, I know" Ironically, the more sure you are ("I know I can't do that"; "I know he would never do that to me"; "I know that I'll make a lot of money on this project"), the more likely you are to be in error.

Third Umpire Characteristics: You know your experience is directly related to the way you label a situation. Kids can play ball all day long without anyone calling balls or strikes. A pitch is a pitch. Each is an opportunity. An event is simply an event until you label it, and you can choose your own labels. You can decide how you want to call your game. When the second umpire says, "I call them as they are," he is confusing a higher level of abstraction (his label about the pitch) with a real event (the pitch itself). The third umpire's perspective ("They aren't anything until I call them") is helpful because here you know you are adding a label (psychological world) onto what is happening (physical world). When you understand that you create much of your life experiences by your choices, you can learn to create labels that will be helpful to you.

Instead of focusing on what might be the "right" label, you use labels that will help you create your vision. A re-label is not a euphemism. Euphemisms are used to cover up current reality. Re-labeling helps you see more of reality, not less. Once you see more of reality you are in a better position to create what you want.

Once you start to think in terms of choice instead of change, you discover that you can label current reality to your advantage. You can immediately create a different psychological experience without immediately changing the physical world. Evaluate your labels by their results. You may find that a particular label will be helpful at one time, and not helpful at another. Ask yourself, does this label serve my vision of what I want to have happen in my life or not?

You can easily move beyond obstacles by re-labeling, because most obstacles are caused by labeling in the first place. Use the following guidelines to help you learn to call your own game by choosing your own labels.

Guidelines for re-labeling

Look for the opportunity in the problem, and then re-label it in a positive way. Positive labeling leads to greater acceptance. "A dull evening with my in-laws" becomes "a chance to learn to raise my emotional tone." See the problem as a gift.

Use bird's eye view labels. Take a step back from the problem and gain perspective before re-labeling it. One man felt shame and guilt for owing back taxes. The big picture was that holding on to the money did help him start his business, so he re-labeled his back taxes as "an unauthorized but well-deserved small business loan from the government." A woman re-labeled her lingering illness as "an opportunity to let my children learn to be more self-reliant."

Give the problem a friendlier name. Psychologist John Enright has written about re-labeling and gives some examples: "Temper outburst against my children" for one person was renamed "dynamic limit setting." "Procrastination" was renamed "willingness to find out by inaction what really needs to be done."

Make the label personal. In each situation, look for a label that has special meaning to you. Enright reports that for one person, "lazy" was renamed "finding out through inaction what needs to be done" and for another person with a more mystical frame of mind, "surrendering to the Tao."

Try many different labels for each situation, then use the one that means the most to you. You could, for example, rename a painful experience (being fired) as "a way to learn humility," "being in the here-and-now," "testing social limits," "creative social engineering," or "expanding my social image."

Look at the situation objectively and positively. Describe it to yourself. Find the positive function it can have in your life. If you have a trait others call "being a miser," you might rename it "financial responsibility."

Many people suffer from what psychologist Dan Dunne calls "AA," or adjective addiction. Your favorite adjectives are chock-full of negative meanings ("I'm flaky," "I'm lazy," "I'm ugly"). Your addiction to negative adjectives keeps you depressed. A helpful technique is to review a negative experience, such as failing an exam, in an objective and positive way. Do this in the third person ("Bill is someone who wants to get ahead; he's sincere about his career; he has a desire to be excellent; he is willing to face current reality").

Go back to the time in the past when you first developed the problem, and find the initial positive role it played in your life. Smoking may first have served as a way to express your independence, drinking alcohol as a way to enjoy the ambience of a party. You may want to quit smoking and drinking, but you do not need to hate yourself because you smoke and drink.

Re-label the problem in terms of the balance it plays in your life. Nearly all problems balance out other potential problems. Failure balances out narcissism, anger balances out fear, and shame balances out pride. You rarely want to get rid of your problem altogether; it usually plays some important role in your life. Try to identify the advantage of one label over another.

Look for ways in which experience expands your awareness. You can come out of any adversity better for the experience. You might feel more empathic to others, or more aware of your own humanity.

Find some other use for the experience. An advantage to being a therapist, or a writer, is that all experiences, negative or positive, can be used in work. Most people can use most of their experiences in some way as well. It makes a good story, if nothing else.

See how the experience could help others. You can use your experience to show others how to avoid the problem, or how to cope with it, if it should happen to them. Theresa Saldana has turned her painful experience as the victim of an attempted murder into a force to help others by founding <u>Victims for Victims</u>, an organization that helps victims of crime.

Re-label the problem as a "learning experience." To learn from a problem, look blamelessly at what you may have done to bring the situation about. The lessons you learn from adversity help you prevent it from happening again. The lesson may be something crucial to your development. If you don't learn it now, the problem will reappear until you learn what you need to know. Suppose you have a bad attack brought on by stress, poor appetite, and lack of exercise. What have you learned? Your suffering can now help you learn to avoid more suffering later. In order to avoid a repetition of the attack, you need to inform yourself about nutrition, exercise, stress reduction and then create a new life-style accordingly. Terry Cole Whitaker says "Mother Nature loves us so much she keeps presenting to us those lessons we need to learn, over and over, until we get them right. Try to identify what the lesson is that you need to learn; learn it.

Question the usefulness of your labels. Your beliefs generate your labels. Keep in mind that the beliefs that lead to depressive labels are formed when you are trying to change others, so that they'll make you happy. Change system labels ("I need to have approval at all times from all people") are useless, whereas choice system labels ("I can enjoy others' approval, but I don't need it") work for you, and they work for what you want in life.

Re-label others

That which rubs you wrong in others is usually a reflection of yourself. If you're overly critical, people who are critical will bother you. To become more accepting of you, accept others by re-labeling the other person's problem. Redeeming qualities in a label make the problem more acceptable. As a result, you hopefully will accept that quality in yourself as well.

How to create self-esteem

Self-esteem is self-acceptance. You project onto others what you cannot accept in yourself. One way to get self-esteem is to build up yourself and your achievement to match your idea of what you should be. A more effective and lasting method is to accept yourself as you are right now, and hold onto the vision of what you want. You accept what you have created in the past. The past is a closed issue; what you can create in the future is wide open.

When your self-esteem is high, you forget about yourself, the world, and the future; you're in the flow. What you do has its own intrinsic rewards, and you're doing it because you choose to do it, not to make you a "worthy" person. You are too busy creating and savoring a good life to ruminate about whether you are a wonderful person or not.

You will develop a greater sense of self as you use the choice principles. You will also help your self-acceptance by acknowledging and accepting certain "resistance traits" and moving beyond them. Ask yourself the following questions, and if you answer yes, ask yourself if you can let go of the trait and focus on something higher.

Am I a perfectionist? (You are rarely satisfied, and may rationalize your dissatisfaction.)

Do I nag? (You continually reprimand and criticize others. You need others to do what you want them to do, so that you'll feel better.)

Am I rude? (You interrupt people, and you are openly impatient with how they express themselves; you reject them as they are, and you need them to act in a certain way for your sake.)

Am I am bigot? (You judge people according to race, religion, sex, age, social class, and other differences; you need people to be just like you to feel good about yourself.)

Am I anxious? (You worry about what might happen. You refuse to accept that the future is unknown and uncertain, and you don't trust your ability to deal with the unknown.)

Do I always wait for things to happen? (You wait for someone to write, visit, or call because you don't feel capable of doing it yourself.)

Do I obsess? (You ruminate about past wrongs because you believe that they cause your present depression.)

Am I over involved? (You meddle in others' lives. You try to change others for the better and reject them as they are.)

Am I a hypocrite? (You pretend you are something you're not because you don't like what you are.)

Do I over monitor? (You watch other people's every move like a hawk, and you refuse to accept their actions for fear you may be "done wrong.")

Do I check and recheck? (You continually double-check your thoughts, feelings, and actions to try to avoid blame.)

If you recognize any one of these traits in yourself, let go of it by accepting it, by choosing to envision the result you want, and by taking action to create it. Don't worry too much about resolving problems, just move on to something better.

Self-acceptance gives you choices

Self-acceptance ("I'll accept myself even though I've lost my job") plus accepting available choices ("One of my choices isn't having that job") equals increased choices (What job options do I have?"). You begin to see new choices all around you as soon as you stop fighting the loss.

One of your choices is to state what you want ("By the first of next month, I want a job that I enjoy that pays $25,000 a year, and has good benefits"). When you accept yourself, you are free to take the offensive. Because you don't ruminate on being a loser, you can move toward your vision ("I lost the job, but I'm still me and I accept myself").

Self-acceptance aligns you with reality

Your success (getting what you want) depends on how good you are at self-acceptance. To create your own life, you have to take yourself as you are, and stop demanding exchanges and refunds ("I'll be happy, if I can just lose weight"). Self-acceptance aligns you with reality and with who you really are ("My vision is to be thin, but I can be happy even with the extra weight"). You start flowing with Mother Nature rather than swimming against the current. When you go with the flow, you can maneuver yourself to where you want to go.

Self-acceptance is taking in information

Self-acceptance is mentally taking in information ("I made a mistake") so that you can use the information to get what you want. You can use the information as a current building block, or you can put it in your memory for later use.

Acceptance happens at a concrete, mechanical level. You become wiser. Often all you have to do to overcome the obstacle is to take in (accept) the information. For example, accepting that you have a medical problem often begins the cure.

The more you know about something, the easier it is to deal with. Fighting the symbolic implication of the information ("This means no one likes me-how could they?") stops you from taking in the information. This is why getting the facts is helpful. By taking in (accepting) information about yourself, you are adjusting your view of reality. You end up having a clearer picture. Even if you dislike the information you receive, you are still in a better position to get what you want. Clarity equals creative ability.

When you create your life by choice, you focus on what exists for you. You agree that it exists even if you disagree with it. What you accept is your reality-what you perceive ("I am overweight"), what you use ("This is my job"), and what you act upon ("This is what I did"). Anything that influences you and anything that you influence is part of your reality—your thoughts and feelings are your reality.

You can go in two directions: toward reality, or away from reality. The further you move away from what is ("I can't stand this"), the more powerless and distressed you are.

Self-acceptance opens new avenues

When you stop trying to fight or right yourself, new doorways open. The father of one of my colleagues was diagnosed as having inoperative metastatic cancer. The family was concerned about telling him this news, but when he was given the information, his response was, "okay, what can we do about it?" Three months later, following a new experimental therapy that he was given, he was free of cancer and doing fine-perhaps in part because of his attitude (his acceptance helped open the door to treatment).

We have often seen that once a person accepts reality, new avenues begin to appear as if out of the blue. The woman who accepts the possibility that she may never get married unexpectedly meets her future husband. The man who accepts losing a job finds a better one. The woman, who could not get pregnant, suddenly is pregnant. They become more open to the opportunities that are always there.

Self-acceptance Is enlightening

With self-acceptance, you don't blame yourself, or judge yourself morally. Your evaluations of your experiences are simply descriptive of current reality. You are free to say what you like, and don't like, but you don't engage in contempt, or moral judgments.

Acceptance is illuminating; a cognitive enlightenment. You see the light. Psychologist Abraham Maslow found in his well-known studies that mentally healthy people have an absence of moral judging. He described them as "non-comparative" and "non-judgmental. "The more mature a person, the more accepting the person."

Moral judgments foster resentment. The harsher your moral judgments ("I'm stupid", "I'm to blame"; "I acted like a fool"), the harsher your feelings (humiliation, disgust, despair). One of the ways to be more accepting is to stop making moral judgments of your experience and to describe them objectively instead. "I am not a bad person; I am only a person who can make mistakes."

Self-acceptance is enlightening. With self-acceptance, you don't blame yourself morally, or judge yourself. Your evaluations of your experiences are simply descriptive of current reality. You are free to say what you like, and don't like, but you don't engage in contempt, or moral judgments.

Self-acceptance is right now

When you're not resisting what happened six days, six months, or six years ago, you're up to date. Self-acceptance allows you to enjoy the present.

Being up to date (not worrying about the past or the future) feels inherently good. To experience the eternal present moment, accept the now—including who you are—as it is: complete and total.

Self-acceptance is feeling good

When you talk about being "up" or "down," you're really talking about being in, or out, of acceptance. When you're in a state of self- acceptance, you feel up; when you're out of it, you feel down.

When you reject any part of the universe (yourself included), you reject all of it. All emotional distress has this feeling of separation, of being cut off and isolated. Acceptance allows you to reconnect and feel part of the universe again.

Paradoxically, by accepting you are responsible for yourself, you feel closer to others ("I can be myself because I don't have to worry about the person hurting me. I don't have to put any walls up"). When you accept the responses you make, and acknowledge the choice of responses you have, you accept yourself: "I accept the fact that I responded to the party by overeating and overdrinking. I acknowledge that I have new choices today. I can eat only when I'm hungry, and only what I want."

"I accept the responses I made to my boss when I was upset. I acknowledge the new choices I have today and that I can create the good relationship I want with him."

Your good moods will let you know whether you're moving toward, or away from, self-acceptance, because you feel good when you accept yourself.

Self-acceptance ascends toxic beliefs

When you accept yourself, you are able to rise above the beliefs that keep you from getting what you want. You adopted many of your beliefs when you were a child, and you had trouble thinking logically. That's why many beliefs contain logical errors; they have a Catch 22 feature that puts you in a no-win situation. You may, for example, have trouble finishing jobs.

These examples are related to housecleaning, but the thinking patterns apply to most other tasks, like writing important reports at the office or finishing academic assignments:

> "I can't do the housework because I have too much housework to do."
>
> "I can't clean the house, because I might find I can't do it."
>
> "I can't clean the house, because I am worthless; I'm worthless, because the house is dirty."
>
> "I can't clean the house, because I didn't clean the house earlier."
>
> "I can't clean the house, because I don't like myself; I dislike myself, because I don't clean the house."

"I can't clean the house, because then it will get dirty again."

"I can't clean the house, because I can't do it the way I want to do it; I can't clean the house, because then I would feel stupid for not having done it before."

"I can't clean the house, because I'm depressed; you know why I'm depressed."

"I can't clean the house, because I might like doing it; then I will want to do it again."

"I can't clean the house, because a dirty house makes me feel disorganized."

"I can't clean the house, because I can't work in a dirty place."

Accepting yourself frees you to do what needs to be done to get you what you want ("I accept the reality that the house is dirty, and that I don't want to clean it, but I have a vision of a clean house, and I will take steps to achieve that vision"). Because you don't spend energy on fighting who you are, you have more energy to create what you want.

Positive beliefs can also block acceptance ("I'm smarter than others"; "I'm always nice"; "I never make big mistakes"; "I'm always good to those I care about"; "I'm always honest"). You may, for example, reject the non-noble thoughts, unpleasant feelings, and non-brilliant actions that go against your ideal image. Because your positive images clash with what you are really doing, you don't tell yourself the truth. When you accept yourself, including your imperfections, you see who you truly are, and you can be honest with yourself.

Self-acceptance is being accountable

You are free from excuses. You own your choices and their consequences. When you are accountable, you don't need excuses ("I have a bad back"; "I didn't get any support"; "I don't have enough money").

The unproductive, unrewarding change system is the excuse system. You place the cause of your experiences outside of you. No matter what goes wrong in your life, you always have an outside hook to hang it on ("The alarm didn't go off." "I had blisters." "No one told me").

In the choice system, the causes of your experiences are within you. You know that at any moment you can create the experience you want by using the ACT Formula:

> Accept current reality.
> Choose and envision the experience you want to have.
> Take action to get it.

Self-acceptance is freedom

It detaches you from what you've been resisting, and, therefore, frees you from it. Have you ever worn eyeglasses? The first few days you see the outline of the rims, and you feel the weight on your nose. At some point, you accept the glasses and stop thinking about them. The same process happens in all acceptance decisions: After putting what you have been resisting to rest, you stop thinking about it. You are free from it.

Separate the choice world from the change world

If you want to understand the differences between choice and change, you need to know that you live in your own unique psychological world, but you share a common physical world with everyone else. Each world has its own separate principles and characteristics. For example, choice is an attribute of the psychological world, and change is a characteristic of the physical world.

You can get rapid relief from emotional distress when you separate the physical from the psychological ("The deal went sour, but I don't have to feel sour"). The two worlds are different; yet, they do coexist, and they do influence each other.

Two different worlds: physical and psychological

The physical world is a world of things that occupy space: your body, your house, and your neighbors. The psychological world is beyond space and time, and it consists of your being, feelings, and experiences. The physical world is finite, and it has limits and boundaries. The psychological world is limitless, and it has no boundaries except the limits of our imagination.

The psychological world exists independently from the physical world. If someone hits you, you feel physical pain: cause and effect. When someone says something unpleasant to you, however, you may, or may not, feel psychological pain: no cause and effect. If your husband, or wife, says, "You're really thoughtless," for example, this hurts you psychologically only if you resist it (need to change it). You cause yourself emotional pain by mixing the two worlds—by attempting to change, or resist, something that can't be changed.

Therapists would become obsolete, and about 90 percent of mankind's psychological pain would be eliminated, if everyone understood the implications implicit in the following two proverbs: "Sticks and stones may break my bones but words will never hurt me," and "The wounds from sticks and stones will heal, but those from words may never."

Each of us adds emotional coloring to our world. Each person in a group often experiences the same event differently. A Republican and Democrat can hear the same speech and each come away more positive than ever that his, or her, point of view is correct. What you tell yourself about an event is what determines your psychological experiences. You can't see the psychological world; you can only experience it. You can attempt to understand another's psychological world through empathy, but you can't ever be sure that what you experience is what others experience. This fact makes empathy a tricky condition.

Your senses often fool you. Your sense of sight, for example, tells you that objects have color even though scientists have proven that objects are colorless. Your eyes have tiny cones in the retinas that color objects. People who are colorblind (their retinas don't have these cones) see objects closer to their true nature.

Similarly, you color events emotionally ("That speech was terrible"; "That show was wonderful") and then see the coloring you have added as if it were part of the event and a cause of your feelings ("He made me mad"; "The show made me happy").

We have an extensive and concrete language to describe the physical world, but we have a limited vocabulary for the psychological world. We usually use physical metaphors to describe the psychological world ("I feel like a million bucks"). These metaphors often cause problems: "I feel worthless. Dirt is worthless. Therefore, I'm dirt"; "Physically you can hurt me. I feel hurt."

Freud's concepts of the psyche were "structural" and "topographic" constructions. He tried to understand the psychological world using physical world conceptualizations. Unfortunately, many who have followed Freud have attempted to do the same thing. In my opinion this is directly related to why this approach may take years to see a result.

Physical principles—-change, work, time, effort, control, avoidance, permanency—cause problems when you try to use them in your psychological world. Pain in your physical world is helpful in that it teaches us to avoid harm (you learn to keep your hands out of the fire). Your coexisting psychological world gives you the awareness and choice to avoid physical pain ("I know that if I stick my hand in the fire I'll get burned, so I'll choose not to"). You want to avoid physical pain. But when you avoid confronting psychological issues out of fear of pain, you often create serious problems for yourself. For example, if you avoid the anxiety of driving after you've had an automobile accident, you'll create a phobia.

As previously stated, the attributes of the two worlds often are opposites: When you give away something physical (possessions, money, land) you have less, but when you give away something psychological (love) you create more within yourself. You can give away something physical (donate money to a worthy cause) and psychologically feel expanded. Many people operate from the physical world perspective, and they can only see that when they give away something, they have less. They resist sharing, because they have not learned they can have a good psychological feeling when giving something away. The more you understand the psychological universe, the faster you can create emotional relief.

Five important facts about your psychological world:

> You run your psychological world.

> Knowledge and awareness expand your psychological world.

> You expand your psychological world by Focusing Outside of Yourself

> Your psychological world can conjure up images of everything that exists or could exist in the physical world.

> When you identify your psychological self with the physical world, or with others' psychological world, you become vulnerable to emotional distress.

You run your psychological world

Others, and events, can influence you psychologically, but they can never dominate you unless you let them. (eg. Stephen Hawking) You are always in charge because you are one hundred percent (100%) responsible for your psychological world: your thoughts, your feelings, and your actions.

You expand your psychological world through knowledge and awareness.

In the choice system you see your current reality as a source of information (feedback), rather than as something you must change and control. For example, if someone tells you, "I don't like the way you look," you regard it simply as information, or feedback. You waste energy if you try to change what the other person said. Whether, or not, you alter how you look is your choice. Mother Nature is constantly giving us feedback that we do not understand the significance of, because we are bent on changing it, rather than understanding it. (Hurt, dissatisfaction, and depression are often Nature's feedback that we should not be doing what we are doing. Because we desire to change our experience, we miss out on understanding the information we are getting).

More gain, less effort

Understanding psychological principles can be more effective in creating what you want in both worlds than understanding physical world principals alone. Those areas in life where you are most successful are the ones where you're using correct psychological principles.

You expand your psychological universe by focusing outside of yourself.

You obtain knowledge, the fuel of your psychological world, by paying attention to others and paying attention to the physical world. When you focus solely on yourself, you narrow your perspective. This is why a good way to overcome depression (a state of destructive self absorption) is to get interested in the outside world.

We humans have evolved and survived, because of our ability to master the physical world: build shelters, grow food, and conquer disease. Nature has biologically wired us to feel good when we master the physical world, and to feel bad when we acquiesce to the forces of the physical world. You master the physical world by directly confronting it at times and by yielding to it at others.

One of the easiest ways to feel better, when you're feeling down, is to master a piece of the physical world: wash your car, get a haircut, clear out a closet, write a letter, or clean off your desk. To master the physical world, you need to focus on it and connect with it by taking action. Once you do this with one or two small tasks, you usually begin to feel connected to the world and others. You feel that you are in the flow, and you are ready for larger tasks.

To create the physical world you want, you need to connect and cooperate with others. You influence others, and you allow them to influence you. This is a dynamic process. You are either expanding personally, and thereby influencing your corner of the physical world, or you're being constricted and pushed around by the physical forces you encounter.

The more of the physical world you can influence and shape, the more you will be reinforced by society. Doctors (not psychiatrists), plumbers, bakers, painters get paid for changing the physical world.

You usually like your physical world (house, job, neighborhood) when you feel like a winner. And you usually dislike the physical world when you feel like a loser ("I hate this farm ... dirty house ... overwhelming job"). We are biologically set up to win by being internally rewarded for creating what we want.

The ultimate aim is to create the psychological and physical worlds that you want. To do so it is necessary to use psychological principles (choice, acceptance, self accountability, awareness of current reality) when dealing with the psychological world, and it can also produce good benefits when used to address much of the physical worlds.

Your psychological world can conjure up images of everything that exists or could exist in the physical world.

Psychological imagery has its advantages and disadvantages. You can imagine disturbing scenarios ("What if I'm attacked?") that frighten, depress, and enrage you; you can then react to the images as if they were real, become upset, and forget all about creating your vision. It is as if the physical world has a fifth column that can defeat you through propaganda ("Why even try? Look at all the things that could happen to you").

The advantage of your imagery is that you can create visions of what you want to happen even before you know how to make it happen. Your imagery helps to provide you with the how. It gives you a blueprint. Your imagery also provides you with an impetus to move toward the vision, as if the images were a magnet pulling on you.

Identifying Your Psychological Self in the Physical World

The psychological world is where the source of vulnerability and emotional distress originate. Your psychological self is pure experience, or being. The most accurate definition of your psychological self is "I am." The psychological world is about being, the physical about having. When you start to add traits from the physical world to your self-identity, you develop problems ("I am my car, my job, my house, my body, my family, my bank account"). If something happens to the physical reality—you get fired, get sick, and lose your money—you take it as an assault on your psychological set.

To create the desired life, you have to let go of errors, traumas, setbacks, bad patches, and misadventures. You stop identifying with them and move on.

The most useful set of principles

Because your psychological universe and physical universe coexist, many situations use both physical principles (change, work, time, force, effort, control) and psychological principles (choice, awareness, and acceptance). For example, learning Russian is both psychological and physiological. You use some biochemical means to store and recall the language, yet you would also have to use psychological means (choosing to study grammar, choosing to memorize vocabulary words) to learn the language.

In the same way, emotional distress is both physical and psychological. However, except in rare cases (manic-depressive psychosis, schizophrenia) where drugs are helpful, psychological principles are the best way to eliminate emotional distress. Even in physiological disorders the correct psychological approach can be very helpful.

Psychological principles are quicker and more effective in creating the experiences you want. If you think only from the perspective of the physical world, you believe that to create a different experience you have to put time and effort into changing ("I've got to change how I feel").

If you want to change something in the physical world, you must generally look for three items: tools, time, and energy. For example, if you decide to change the desk at which you are writing into a chair (physical principles), you will need an array of tools such as a saw, hammer, square, glue, screws, drills, sandpaper, and so forth. You would need some time (especially if you are not much of a carpenter) and you would spend a lot of energy before the job was completed. Actually, as you look around, you probably can see several hundred places in the room where you could sit, so perhaps you will choose to use one of those for the time being. The choice you make is based on a psychological principle that will save you many problems and much time in the physical world.

Patients are sometimes shocked by the answer they get when they come into my office telling me, "I have come to get some tools, so I can change the problem I am dealing with." My response is, "You can get tools at a hardware store; I don't have any here. I am also not in the change business, so you will not find that here either."

No matter how bad you feel, you can get relief with choice. Even if your current reality remains the same, you can make a snap decision to enjoy yourself or choose to snap out of a funk in a moment. Nothing in your physical world may change, but you can create a different experience. Rather than trying to change your experience make a choice to create a different experience. Victor Frankel, in his book about his concentration camp experiences, observed that one of the things you could see in the concentration camp was people making choices.

The reason patients can get rapid relief from emotional distress is that using psychological principles in the psychological world brings rapid results. If we had to help people change their other circumstances, it would be a different story. In the physical world, things are often cemented together and change takes time. In the psychological world everything is liquid, fluid, and flexible. No matter how distressed patients are feeling when they come, they can leave the office feeling better.

Change means waiting. To get rapid relief, you need to stop thinking of change. The work and time that change requires can psychologically defeat you. Change amounts to very slow relief from emotional distress. It is not a response (thought, feeling, action) you can make. When you want to change something, you have to wait because change is accomplished over time with an expense of energy. When you choose something ("I choose to get along with my mother"), you give your brain instructions for something it can do immediately.

Trying to change something helps maintain the status quo. Change sabotages you in many ways ("I'm going to change tomorrow, and I will never eat junk food again, so I better eat as much as I can tonight"). You are trying to use a physical concept to create a psychological experience ("If I make myself feel guilty enough, I'll change and stop putting off my studies"). Change occurs in the physical world and not in the psychological. The closest attribute to change in the psychological world is habit.

How you become trapped in the change system

The change system's thinking is caused by confusing the physical world with the psychological world; a confusion that is a legacy from childhood. People under use psychological principles, mainly, because they lack awareness of how it operates and how effective it can be. In elementary school, you learned about the physical world. Later you learned abstract facts about the physical world (history, economics) and more sophisticated knowledge of the physical world (physics, chemistry). But there is no specific curriculum that teaches the principles of the psychological world. You first learned about the physical world—that it could be changed and controlled—as a child. You learned how to control your bladder, tie your shoes, coordinate a knife and fork, and use a pencil. Your early success in life depends on mastering such physical world principles. Until you became eleven or twelve years of age, you were developmentally unable to separate the psychological world from the physical world, or to use most of the psychological principles. You used tears and smiles to get your way, and each time you succeeded it reinforced the basic premise that others are responsible for your experiences, and you are responsible for others.

Developmentally, you needed to think this way when you were a child. You were dependent on others to take care of you, and you needed a way to manipulate them so that they would. In psychological terminology, this self-centered thinking is called parataxic thinking. You tend to believe you're the center of the world and the cause of whatever is going on. In your primary learning years (ages two through eleven) you were basically a parataxic thinker.

In childhood blame felt right. Parataxic thinking is why as a child, you blamed yourself when something went wrong, such as your parents' fighting, drinking, divorcing, or dying. You used a frame of reference that confused the physical world with the psychological. As a result, you saw life mainly from a blame perspective ("I got mad at Dad and thought something bad about him; that's why he died"). You thought your feelings (psychological world) were connected to events (physical world), so you blamed yourself or others when events went wrong.

You were developmentally unable to see emotional trauma any other way. You couldn't uncouple bad events from bad feelings ("I broke my toy, so of course I feel bad"). Small children can often distinguish between what they cause, and what is caused by outside forces. However, when something traumatic happens, they have trouble being accountable for their actions, and they want to blame someone else.

A four-year-old can understand he is "blaming" when he is alone, trips, falls down, and says his mother caused it. He can correct this error and see his mother was not present when he fell. However, he needs a higher level of development to have his mother scold him just before he happens to fall and still be able to say his mother was not to blame. If somehow his mother did trip him, it would be nearly impossible for him to see how he was responsible for his psychological feelings about the situation, and for him not blame his mother for his hurt feelings.

As an adult, you have the mental hardware to separate what happens to you physically from how you experience it psychologically. You may, however, be heavily conditioned by your early parataxic thinking processes, and this thinking will often predispose you to the way you feel.

Early in the development of rapid therapy concepts, I saw a young patient who was almost always upset. I had worked with her for several months and had given her numerous interpretations of why she acted the way she did. These helped very little. One day, at my wits' end as to how to help her, I asked how come she always seemed to be so upset. She thought for a moment and said, "If you're not upset, how will people know you care?" Her comment, more than anything else, helped me realize that the way you think determines the way you show your symptoms. Her comment about the relationship between caring and being upset was more revealing than the dynamic formulations I had attempted to put together.

In childhood tying X to Y felt right. In our early learning we glued events and feelings together. For all practical purposes, we saw the event and feeling as inseparable. When you said, "My friend made me mad," you believed that to be completely true. You perceived X (an event) and experienced Y (a feeling) and therefore you concluded that X caused Y. This was how your brain processed information during your early years. As you grew up, you recorded and linked numerous event-and-feeling episodes in your mind, and most of them have probably stayed with you. The process is like an idling motor ready to spring into action at the least excuse.

Why change seems so right

Here are some common questions about change:

"Doesn't the need to change motivate me?"
When you confuse the physical and psychological worlds, you believe you need a strong physical incentive (pain) to get what you want. This is not true when you are operating from the psychological world.

"If I change, won't I permanently solve my problem?"
You may desire change because change implies permanence. You want assurances that you'll never have the problem again, but your struggle to change things only compounds your problem. While some choices ("I'll stop smoking") can last for years, the original choice or option does not

disappear ("I'll have just one cigarette"). Choice doesn't create permanence, but choice is a permanent option.

"Why does change often feel right?"
Change frequently seems right, because it is often an escape fantasy. It seems to take you away from your painful current reality. You want everything to change and be wonderful, so you dream it, and struggle for it. You may believe you can change into a different person ("If I get a job …if I move … if I finish school . . . if I get married ... if I get a divorce... if I retire…"), but you set yourself up for failure, because you are labeling something physical (for example, losing weight) as the cause of something psychological (feeling good).

After some initial success with change strategies ("I've lost weight"; "I've saved some money"), you become disappointed when you realize that you are still the same person. Then you give up on your vision and think, "It must be something else that will make me happy," and you pursue that, continuing to assign the power to make you happy outside of yourself.

"What about changing others for their own good?"
Do you have relatives or friends who are their own worst enemies: a son who drinks too much, a daughter attracted to abusive men, a husband killing himself by smoking two packs a day, a friend pushing others away while suffering from isolation and loneliness? The futility of change is obvious when you look at your efforts to change others.

Change, whether you're trying to change yourself, or others, is lack of acceptance. Change naturally creates resistance. Choice, on the other hand, implies acceptance. You will get much more cooperation if you ask people to make different choices instead of asking them to change.

The more you believe you can change others, the more you feel like a failure. You do, however, indirectly influence others. For example, you can influence others to use a seat belt by using one yourself. One of the best ways to influence people is to do what you want them to do. Being an influence is far different from trying to change someone. We can help increase others' awareness, but we can't change them. If someone decides to be happy, you can't make him or her unhappy. If someone decides to be unhappy, you can't make him or her happy.

"Shouldn't I change what makes me unhappy?"
All patients, in some way, have failed to divide the two worlds. "Rain makes me overeat"; "Rain depresses me", "I was really mad that it had to rain on our vacation"; "Thunder and lightning make me panic." You can easily spot this in others, but it's usually difficult to see in yourself.

You have a powerful means for feeling better
Once you get the hang of separating your psychological experiences from the physical outside events, you possess a powerful means to feel better. Instead of trying to change things, you create the internal experiences you want. You no longer need to operate from the assumption that more of the physical (money, status, or approval) will make you happy ("I can create happiness no matter how much money I have"). You no longer have to operate from the assumption that less of the physical (less weight, fewer hassles, or a simpler life) will make you happy ("I can create peace of mind no matter what the demands of life").

You no longer have to wait to change apartments, to graduate, or to go on vacation to be happy.

You don't have to demand perfection to feel contented ("If I can fly, I'll soar", if I have to crawl, I'll crawl, but I refuse to be unhappy"). You can create separate psychological and physical visions instead of believing that one causes the other. You're better able to create what you want. You can separate what you are responsible for (your psychological world) and what you are not responsible for (the physical world and others' psychological worlds). If people in your physical presence are having bad moods or are not enjoying themselves, you don't have to take personal responsibility for them ("It's a hundred degrees outside and he's in a rotten mood, but I'm choosing to have a good time").

It is useful to understand that these two worlds coexist, so that you can cause them to move in the same direction. When you decide to do something, rather than go physically, yet resist psychologically ("I'll go to the movie with him, but I'll hate every minute of it"), you can decide to be fully there. You get your thoughts, feelings, and actions going in the same direction. You don't have to be devastated by physical traumas once you separate the two worlds ("Okay, I've been diagnosed as having cancer. This is a fact, but how I respond to the diagnosis psychologically is up to me").

Choice creates experiences: you can start whining

When you learn to divide the two worlds, you have already won. You come to recognize that few things in the physical world can cause you to feel emotional pain. What you choose to believe will have consequences, and you can create the consequences you want by choosing what to believe. How you choose to see an event is up to you. You can see it in one way ('It's awful!"), or another ("It's great!"), but what you choose creates your experiences. You can choose to believe in honesty or dishonesty, in love or hate, in goodwill or ill will, in your worth or worthlessness, in manipulation or cooperation.

Even with the death of a loved one, you can get relief from emotional pain by understanding that pain is a product of need, and choosing acceptance relieves psychological pain.

The power of psychological principles was demonstrated in what happened between the United States and China in 1972. Almost overnight, twenty-five years of entrenched, at times violent animosity, between the two countries, was eliminated. The leaders accomplished this instant transformation by making one choice: they made up their minds to have good relations despite their policy disagreements. In essence, they used the ACT Formula.

> They Accepted their differences.
> They Chose to have good relations.
> They Took action to work out the details.

The current reality—that there are differences between the United States and China—did not change. Yet this one decision had far-reaching ramifications—from the price of tea in China to whom Americans cheered for in the 1984 Olympics.

If the United States and China had tried to use physical principles (change, control, force) to solve their problems, hostility between the two countries would still exist. This use of the ACT Formula is not an isolated one. Anwar Sadat's decision to visit Israel in 1979 created a similar rapid shift in international relations. Because psychological principles can so easily and effortlessly create a completely different experience, the results can seem as almost miraculous.

Choices create your life

This is cause and effect. What you choose is what you sow; when you die, your life will be the sum of all of your choices. You are always your own worst enemy, or your own best friend.

Responsibility and self-accountability

When we attempt to examine our choices, one confusing word keeps emerging. The reasons it is confusing is that everyone thinks they know what the word means, but there is little actual agreement between people about its meaning. In my office I may get as many as 20 answers to the question, "Who is <u>responsible</u> for this pencil staying on my desk?"

The meanings used for the word "Responsibility" contain two opposing ideas. Being nearly opposite and never being clarified, this naturally leads to confusion. Because the word is used so often everyone thinks they know what is being said, but there is no guarantee that the person hearing it has the same idea in mind as the person saying it.

"RESPONSIBILITY"

Response ability	Assigned Accountability

One of the meanings contained in the word "responsibility" has to do with the assignment of causality to self or other. For example: "I'm responsible for my parent's fights, and their fights are responsible for my feelings." This meaning of the word is best understood as assigning accountability to someone, or something. Attorneys like to assign accountability for events to "fill their pockets." "He is your patient, and sure he made the decision to kill himself, but you have insurance, and the family and I want money for the fact that you couldn't stop him." In all of these examples, the use of the word responsibility is an attempt to advance the assignment of accountability.

The dictionary meaning of responsibility helps confuse people. It also helps to confuse the approaches needed to deal with the physical and psychological worlds.

When critiquing physical events, we often express the belief we have caused them. If you run over someone with your car you will be seen as responsible for hurting the person. If you shoot off a gun in your neighborhood and the bullet hits a person, you will be seen as the responsible person, even though the bullet released from the gun did the actual damage. In the physical world there is often a causal relationship between the events—the bullet would not have caused the damage if the person had not done something to cause the gun to fire.

Unfortunately, when we use the word "responsible" here, what we are really talking about is assigning accountability. It would make more sense if we actually dealt with it the way it happens.

The car killed the pedestrian. The person being held accountable for the car's behavior is the driver. Mitigating circumstances could be that it was foggy, the road was slippery and the man who was hit jumped in front of the car in a suicidal attempt. It is too simplistic to say the driver is "responsible" for the event.

A person shoots a gun off into the air and someone is injured. The bullet caused the injury. The man is responsible and accountable for shooting off the gun. Why? The law (Shannon's Law) says so. In fact, just discharging the gun is against the law. This is an example of physical world event, causing a physical world consequence.

The relation between sequential events ("You criticized me, and I feel bad.") is seldom if ever directly casual. When you try to tie the two worlds together without understanding, you can create guilt, shame, and low self-esteem, but you do not make a case for causality.

The dictionary definition of responsibility keeps people confused. For many people responsibility means being blamed, or being in trouble. The dictionary meanings of responsibility creates a sense of burden that people try to avoid ("Who's responsible here?" "Not me!") It is confusing. The teenager says, "My parents won't let me be responsible for anything," and his parents say, "He won't accept responsibility for anything." This confusion just keeps resolution out of arms reach. It contributes to people feeling helpless and hopeless. ("There's nothing I can do. I'm not responsible for what happens to me.") Thinking of responsibility this way keeps you stuck. ("I can't accept the death of my son, because I feel responsible"). You often end up feeling helpless and hopeless ("There's nothing I can do; I'm not responsible for what happens to me").

There are several attributes of response ability. (A subtype of "responsibility")

Response ability is ability plus awareness. If a blind man is given the job of turning on the lights at dusk, there may be a problem. He can do the job; he may not know when dusk occurs, however. The quadriplegic given he same job has a different problem. He may know when dusk occurs, but he will not be able to do the job. With each, their ability to respond is limited by either awareness or ability.

This has another side. If you are walking down the sidewalk and there is trash on the ground, you have the response ability to pick it up. You have both the awareness and the ability. If you come home after a hard day's work and find the house a mess, you have response ability for cleaning it up.

In any given situation many people may have response ability for doing something. Theoretically, we can all give to any number of charities. We could all spend time cleaning up the neighborhood. If we all tried to take care of all the things we have response ability for, we would probably never be able to get out of the house. It must become apparent that none of us deal with all of the things we have response ability to do. The important thing here is to recognize that we have response ability in many situations. We should not attempt to shrug it off, or to exploit others because we overlap in areas of response ability. Each person must decide which of the things they have response ability for. It works best when we are clear about what we can do something about.

It is important to recognize that response ability is constantly in flux. If I have a pencil in my hand, I have almost 100% of the say about how the pencil is to be used. If I lay the pencil down, perceivably, I could loose all ability to determine how it will be used in seconds. If I am at the pool, I can monitor what is happening at the pool. If I fall asleep, or walk inside, I may find I have no idea about what is happening poolside. The speed at which our ability to do something can change is often under-appreciated by people. A child is in a pool; there is a distraction, and then there is a dead child.

Response ability is the workhorse. It has to do with causality. It is about what one can do without other's participation. It is mine. It is yours. No one can give it to me. Either I have it, or I do not have it. I cannot take it from someone else, and I cannot give it to anyone else. In other words, response ability is intrinsic. It is inseparable from the situation as well as being inseparable from the person. It cannot be transferred!

Let me explain. I am a doctor. I cannot give my abilities to anyone else. I have a friend who is an electrician. He cannot give me his ability. These are intrinsic aspects of the person. What if my electrician friend were to come upon an auto accident where people were hurt? The need intrinsic to the situation is that someone has to help the injured people, or get them help. The need is intrinsic to the situation. What my friend could do varies with what is available at the scene. If there were a first aid kit, he could perhaps do more than if there were no supplies. What he would be response able for is what ever he could do. He would use the knowledge he has, and he would apply it to the situation as best he could. He might draw from memories of shows on television, or first aid courses he took in the past.

His response would be a summation of the intrinsic features in himself and in the situation. Thanks to lawyers and litigious individuals, many doctors will no longer stop and help victims of an accident; this is because they don't want to spend the next five years in court trying to prove they did the best they could under the circumstances. These unwanted experiences led to doctors being more inclined to stop and call their attorney for advice (which would probably be to "pass on by") than to render care. Good Samaritan Laws have helped in most states.

An attribute of response ability is that it is not transferable, and it should not be assignable, unless it is intrinsic. I will discuss accountability in more detail later, but it should be understood that assigning responsibility is really an assignment of accountability and not response ability. You should not assign response ability for the same reasons responsibility cannot be transferred. It is intrinsic. If it is not intrinsic, it really does not exist. Lawyers, on the other hand, do this all the time, because the ordinary person does not understand this quality of response ability.

What the universe seems to do best is to change. In the same way response ability is constantly in transition. What I can do at one moment may not be possible a moment later. What I could not do yesterday may be possible to do today. Just getting up and moving from one place to another alters the entire range of what <u>was</u> possible, and movement alone can open up a whole new book of what <u>is</u> possible.

I said initially that response ability is awareness plus capability. This means that if our awareness increases, so does our response ability. If our capability increases, so does our response ability. These are a part of our intrinsic picture. Capability may mean an intellectual aspect or a physical aspect. Awareness may mean knowledge or experience.

There are other items that may determine outcome in a given situation. The man with the 45-caliber pistol in his hand may have more to say about what goes on in a room than those without such a devise. The man with a backhoe may be able to get the pool dug faster and cleaner than the man without equipment, but may have the same level of accountability.

You may have already figured out that a lot of people may have overlapped response ability. Each brings their unique intrinsic aspects to any situation, or condition. In any given situation each person owns their unique perspective.

Let me restate a few obvious things about response ability:

> Anyone who has the ability to respond in the here-and-now has response ability, but only to the level of their awareness.
> Response ability is different from blame, intent, or right-or-wrong.
> Response ability is part of a given situation, and it is inseparable from it.
> Each person is response able for his or her own feelings, thoughts and actions.
> Response ability is affected by inner and outer influences
> Response ability is limited or expanded by awareness.
> Response ability is not obligation, or duty.
> Response ability is not control.
> Response ability doesn't mean capacity; it means capability plus awareness.
> One cannot take, give, or transfer response ability, because it is intrinsic.
> It does not mean doing what a parent asks.

IN SUMMARY THERE ARE ONLY THREE THINGS THAT WE ARE RESPONSE ABLE FOR: OUR OWN THOUGHTS, OUR OWN FEELINGS, AND OUR OWN ACTIONS.

Let's turn to accountability, the second concept under responsibility. We can talk about assigned accountability and self-accountability. Self-accountability is an assignment of accountability to one's self. Self-accountability includes what you are directly response able for and what you can indirectly influence.

Accountability is first of all a convention. By this I mean that it is made up. If your car slips out of gear and rolls back into another car, who will they come looking for? If you said the owner of the car, you would likely be correct. The owner could correctly say, "I was not there, I should not be held response able for the accident." The accurate response would be, "That is correct, you are not responsible for the accident, but you are being held accountable for the damage your car caused." This could get more interesting if the owner says, "Actually, I had the car in the garage yesterday for this very problem, and the mechanics told me they had fixed it. I think they should be the ones held accountable for the damage." The lawyers would love this one. They could sue the owner, and then the mechanics for recovery of damages.

Why do women get two or three times the jail sentence for killing a man, then a man gets for killing a woman? Why do we have stupid conventions like, "don't ask; don't tell." All of these are conventions. They are made up to cover a particular issue.

Accountability is different from response ability in all aspects. Accountability is often fixed: Sometimes by law (The board of directors may be the accountable body of a corporation), sometimes by religious convention (The woman is to be obedient to her husband), sometimes by tradition (The Pope must be a man), and sometimes for no real perceivable reason at all (Why should I pick up this mess?).

Accountability is assignable (You watch the kids, while I go to the store), it is not dependent on things like internal, or external factors (The guy with the shovel may be as accountable for the pool getting dug as the guy with the backhoe, and the student with the average IQ may be expected to get as many right answers on a test to get an A as the genius). There is a consideration called diminished capacity. Theoretically under the law children and mentally disabled are not held at the same level of accountability as normal adults. As mentioned before, in this country children are often tried as adults, and the mentally ill are sometimes executed; therefore, one should not rely on that consideration.

Self-accountability includes two possible areas: one is the circle of response ability and the other is the area surrounding responsibility, the area of possible influence. It is useful to accept accountability in the areas where we have all the power. It is often even more important to accept some accountability in the areas of possible influence. These areas are not as fixed as is the area of response ability. It is an area that can be expanded. We can get better at influencing others, and If we work on it, we can find other ways to be an influence. It is like learning to become the best salesman in a car dealership. In the area of possible influence, we are dependent on other's cooperation. I can get good at presenting the pros and cons of buying the car, but, in the end, the person has to be willing to buy, or there is no sale.

Self-accountability helps us learn the relationship between our decisions and the outcomes they create. Blame is an opposite cognition to self-accountability. In blame we place the response ability for what happens in others (person, place, and event). When we do this there is no learning. It is not accurate, so there is nothing to build on. There is no learning curve when we are in blame. In blame we are almost always wrong.

We give up the victim role when we stay accountable. In accountability we seek to understand our role. Whether our role is 10% or 90%, we begin to see how we can alter the outcome. We learn to assume a James Bond attitude toward survival. We are always trying to find the solution to the problem that is presenting itself at the moment. Self-accountability helps you accept reality, because it is objective, concrete, and descriptive of what you did, or what you can do. You're able to see more clearly the relationship between what you do and what happens in your life. Once you hold yourself accountable for what happens to you, you can start getting internal directions on what needs to be done. This is a precursor to building good self-esteem.

Self-accountability influences all areas of your life. No area of your life is unaffected by your degree of self-accountability. You can greatly influence your health when you hold yourself accountable for what you eat, whether or not you exercise, how you relax, whether or not you drink, take drugs, or smoke—all these are within your circle of response ability, and they will have a direct, or indirect, influence on your health. The same can be said for nearly all areas of your life.

Let me restate a few obvious things about accountability:

> Staying in self-accountability, as opposed to blame, is a precursor to developing good self-esteem

> Self-accountability helps ground you in current reality.
> Self-accountability helps you learn cause and effect relationships.
> Accountabilities are often fixed.
> Accountabilities may not be influenced by internal, or external factors.
> Accountability can be transferred, or assigned, to anyone for anything at anytime.
> Self-accountability is not self-blame.
> Self-accountability influences all areas of your life.
> Staying in the choice system can lead to relief for life.

Let's say you play tough tackle football every Saturday afternoon. You hurt. All week long you hurt. Week after week you're in pain. You finally decide to do something to stop the pain. You have three options:

Hang in there, but get upset at yourself for being unable to avoid getting hurt so often.

Hang in there while you get upset at everyone else for playing so rough. Get out of the game entirely, and spend your Saturdays at the beach.

When you believe you need to change reality, you use double-barreled blame—-you blame others and you blame yourself. You are both a victim and an aggressor ("They did it to me, so I'm going to do it back to them").

Needing to change the world is like the football game. You have the same three options:

> Try to change yourself.
> Try to change others.

Quit trying to change the world and use choice to create what you want.

If you've spent your life in the change system, you will find the choice system a whole new universe. The more you get to know it, the more familiar it will become.

Learning to use choice is like learning a new language. First you learn the grammar, or rules of choice ("I'm responsible for my choices, others are responsible for theirs"). You may feel self-conscious and artificial when you begin to use the techniques. But, after you have practiced the choice system for a while, you forget about the basic rules, or grammar, because choice comes naturally. With practice you will become fluent in using choice. Under stress you may regress back to trying to change things, just as an immigrant, who has recently learned a new language, may regress back to the mother tongue.

If you live and work with people who assign accountability for their lives to you, and to others, you may find yourself going back to your old change ways. However, you can quickly bring yourself back to the choice system with the methods given below.

To help yourself let go of change and stay with choice use the following methods:

> Stop rescuing others. Helping and serving others is one of the secrets of leading a happy life. However, helping people who don't want to help themselves serves nobody. Social scientists now believe that this kind of help enables the problem to continue. Experts in fields such as obesity, smoking, alcoholism, delinquency, drug abuse, and emotional disorders believe that your attempts to help people with these problems allow them to continue the problem. The most common pattern is for one person (usually a woman) to take on excessive responsibility for another person (usually a man) who takes little responsibility for himself. She may take on many jobs for the person, such as waking him in the morning and getting him to work. She may take on his emotions for him (feel bad when he messes up). The more she does for him, the less he does for himself. He sleeps late, won't work, and blames his bad feelings on her. If you take on too much responsibility, you are just as unhealthy as the one you are rescuing. You are the mirror opposites of one another—your degrees of immaturity are parallel. If the other person does almost nothing for himself, or herself, and you do almost everything for him, or her, then you are just as psychologically impaired as he, or she, is.

Many people say, "I can't just let the other person go down the drain." This plumbing metaphor is correct—you are caught in a trap. The more you try to pull the other person out of the drain, the more determined the other person is to go down. You do have to let go; that's the only way out of the trap. You must focus on yourself, and you must save yourself. If you don't, ultimately both of you will go down the drain. If you let go, the other person may indeed go down the drain; you have no guarantee that the other person will ever hit rock bottom and start climbing back. But, unless you let go, there is little chance that the person will ever accept reality and start making new choices.

Claudia Repko and Joann Krestan, experts on alcoholism, talk about this in their book *The Responsibility Trap: A Blueprint for Treating the Alcoholic Family*. They suggest that the "co-alcoholic" (the family member trying to help the alcoholic) accept the reality that he, or she, cannot change the alcoholic. The authors believe that once the people around the alcoholic have "hit bottom," and they stop trying to rescue the alcoholic, the alcoholic is likely to "hit bottom," also. They describe hitting bottom for the would-be helper as a process of acceptance, and that the attempt to change another person is doomed to failure.

Letting go of the need to change others is the hard/easy approach. You may have to tolerate some uncomfortable feelings in the beginning, as you stay true to yourself in the face of others' manipulation. Letting go of the need to change others isn't hating the other person, but is detaching for the good of both of you. You can be responsive to other people without being responsible for them. You can, for example, help others out of a sense of choice, as opposed to helping them because you feel responsible for them.

Regard each new encounter with other people as a new experience. Recognize your past patterns so that you become aware of whether, or not, your distress is simply a repeat (from habit) of past experiences. If in the past you responded to manipulation with guilt, you may fall right into it again when you encounter the person who manipulated you. Now that you know about the choice system, choose to discard your old patterns. Make each experience you have a fresh chance to create your life.

Beware of vibes. In a sense, each one of us has a degree of telepathy. We can sense others' emotional states without having rational reasons for doing so. You sense that the other person is angry at you, or that you are in a hostile, unfriendly place. Often the vibes you sense can be a result of your own projection, but often they are true.

Even though you can pick up bad vibes, you may misread them. For example, you visit someone and you sense unfriendly vibes; you speculate that he or she is angry with you when the truth is that the person has been arguing with his, or her, spouse.

Don't take responsibility for others' bad vibes, even if they are blaming you. By using the ACT formula, you can often raise the emotional tone of the situation, and influence other people positively.

Bad vibes can be contagious. If you are entering a "bad vibe" situation, inoculate yourself beforehand ("They are usually into blaming me and others, so I'll stay alert to the choice system while I'm there").

Be aware of manipulation. Many people in authority like to keep you in the change system because it's a way to control you. Some religious groups, governments, judges, police officers, children, and parents can be skillful at manipulating you into believing that you are responsible for making them happy, comfortable, and satisfied.

Often you are unaware of manipulation. Don't let others' facial expressions throw you into the change system. Facial expression is the most common form of manipulation. A face has fifteen pairs of skilled muscles that can be used to show feelings. Facial expressions can be read universally. The more you feel responsible for others' experiences, the more sensitive you will be to facial cues.

When you're being manipulated, the elegant solution is to hold your ground and endure others' displeasure. This may mean holding your tongue when the other person is trying to bait you into a fight, and to speak up when the person expects you to acquiesce. You also have available to you an inelegant, but still useful solution: to leave the situation, or to avoid the situation until you have the courage to be true to yourself.

Model the choice system. Pointing out to others that they are trying to manipulate you often backfires. This heats up the discussion, and before you know it, you're trying to change the other person. Note what happens, for example, in this exchange between a wife and husband:

WIFE (complaining): "Your mother makes me so mad,"

HUSBAND (angrily): "It really makes me mad that you let my mother upset you like that, when are you going to stop letting outside events control your feelings?"

Now see how they could have handled the same situation more satisfyingly by using the choice system:

WIFE (complaining): "Your mother makes me so mad."

HUSBAND: "I find when I'm self accountable around my mother, I feel good, even if she nags me about our children. I could choose never to see her again, but I hold myself accountable for choosing to visit her despite her nagging."

Model what you want: "I find when I'm self-accountable it usually feels good" versus "If you would be responsible for your own life, it wouldn't feel so bad".

Be your own authority. Parents are the first people you feel you need to change. They seem to have all the power, and you feel you have none. Small children's love affairs with guns and superheroes have to do with this sense of powerlessness. In your early experience you deduce that some people seem to be superior, and others seem to be inferior. Your observation is reinforced by cultural distortions (poor people are inferior to rich people; slow kids are inferior to bright kids; athletes are superior to non-athletes; old people are inferior to young people).

People usually feel more responsible for those above them than below them, which is why when you meet a rich, successful person you're more likely to be nervous; you're taking responsibility for them liking you.

Develop a sense of democracy. Actively argue with your tendencies to put people below you, or above you. As you do, you will find that you regard yourself as the equal of all people, and therefore you are your own authority

Choose to be socially free. Whenever you find yourself uncomfortable around other people, ask yourself if you're trying to live up to a social role you believe you should be playing ("I'm the boss/father/lawyer/friend" or "I'm the life of the party/the one who always listens and sympathizes/the follower/the leader"). Make the conscious choice to be free, and to be you. Say and do what feels natural to you at the moment.

Be true to yourself. You would give your life away if you tried to do everything everyone expected of you. Your boss, your parents, your children, your husband or your wife, your friends, and neighbors all expect you, at times, to do what you don't want to do, and not to do what you want to do. To be true to your visions and to create your own life, you sometimes have to go against others' expectations. Be willing to pay the price by knowing that what others think, or say, about you is their business, not yours.

Be willing to let go of the temporary securities and benefits of the change system. Part of your mind wants to hang on to the belief that you need to change yourself, others, and the world. To keep this belief alive, your mind will tell you that if you let go of trying to change or blame, you will lose something important.

The benefits of holding others accountable for your experiences may seem so valuable and necessary that you are afraid to let go of them. Blaming others for your problems lets you off the hook. Blaming others for your feelings seems to offer an apparent advantage in that you can manipulate others, but the benefits are short-term. People may initially do what you want, but eventually they resent you.

When you become accountable for your life, some people may turn away from you, particularly those who like being able to manipulate you. In the long run, however, you'll attract more people to you.

Keep your energy high. You're most likely to go into the change trance when your energy is low. Then you use more energy trying to change current reality, and the problem becomes self-perpetuating. After a good night's sleep, or a few days' rest away from a dilemma, you come back ready to solve it. When your energy is low, your best move is to seek isolation and build up your energy level. Focusing on what you don't want drains energy. Focusing on what you do want creates energy. Eating and sleeping right, and avoiding excesses, can help you keep your energy level up. If you have trouble letting go of your distress, you may be overloading yourself. You may need some balance (more or less work), some time out, or help with your situation, such as hiring a cleaning person.

Care for others in a healthy way. You can care about and help others without taking responsibility for their well-being. Treating others well is usually beneficial to you. If you treat people well, most of the time they will move toward you, and if you're wise, you'll make choices that bring you the types of experiences you want to have. This usually includes the enjoyment of others and their goodwill.

Keep it simple. When you're distressed, you often feel overwhelmed. You think your problems are too complex and too big for any simple solution. No matter how complex a situation may be, you can always make it more complex, or simpler. Accept the reality that you are over whelmed, then look for simple choices that will appear in your current reality.

Keep your feelings in perspective. You may be thrown because your feelings will validate the change system. The choice system, at first try, may not seem to be working for you. Rather than intellectualizing your feelings away or ignoring them, accept them and start moving toward what you want to happen. A by-product of moving toward what you want is good feelings. If you continue to operate from the choice system, your feelings will begin to validate it.

Predict, prepare, and let go. You will probably try to change something in some situations more than in others. You will find it useful to predict how you would handle the situation if you were in the change system, and how you would handle it with choice and creation. Write each potential approach in your notebook. This use of contrasts allows you to preempt the change situation. For example, suppose you were going to talk to your boss about upgrading your job:

Change System
"I'll wait and hope he brings it up."
"I'll try to change him and feel like a failure, if I can't convince him."
"I'll get my feelings hurt, if he disagrees with me."
"I'm afraid I'll hurt his feelings by asking for this."
"I'll resent him for putting me in this position."
"I'll feel helpless, as if he's an adult, and I'm a child."
"If he refuses, I'll feel hopeless about ever getting to do what I want."
"I'll be devastated if he disagrees with me or criticizes me on any point."
"I won't want to tell him what is really on my mind, because I don't want to make him mad."
"I'll end up feeling more isolated and alone."

Choice System
"I'll talk to him the first chance I get."
"I'll see cooperation, not control, or power."
"I'll refuse to feel bad, no matter what happens."
"I'll totally accept myself and the situation."
"I'll choose to be confident, and to be true to myself."
"If we have a difference, I'll acknowledge it, and I will still go for what I want."
"If he refuses to go along with what I want, I'll see what other options I have."
"I'll hold myself accountable for the whole situation."
"I'll learn something from it, no matter what happens."
"I'll keep my eye on the ultimate vision of doing what I want to do and feel free, connected to others, and hopeful."

Once you have written out your two possible approaches and their outcomes, you are in a better position to create what you want. You can preempt (let go of) the change plan and choose the choice plan.

Relief for life

As you have seen, creating your life from choice is something that is always available to you. At first, the choice system may seem artificial, but, in time, it can become second nature. Remember: You don't have to wait to practice until you feel better. As you practice, you will find that you already feel better.

Practice is what makes the choice system seem natural. It is the way in which you lay claim to choice for your life. When you get rapid relief from emotional distress by stepping into the choice system, you may find yourself wishing that you could always use the choice system; always have that kind of miracle available. You can! Living in the choice system gives you relief for life. You always have choices, no matter what situation you are in. When you accept your current reality and choose what you want in life, the choices you need to get there will appear. A whole life is open to you, your life, and you can make it the life you want. When you step from the change system to the choice system, the relief is not only rapid, but it is yours to create for life.

Are you an agile learner?

From time to time, we find ourselves back in the change system and distressed; but we can learn to catch ourselves more rapidly. With focus we are able to move back into creating what we want rather than reacting, and thereby, creating what we do not want.

Successful people have characteristics that enable them to learn the difference between change and choice, and to implement these methods almost immediately.

Can you admit to being wrong? If you can say, "I made a mistake," you will be able to learn to use choice. The best way to learn is to invest in your best awareness, even if it means admitting your mistakes. Can you easily say, "I don't know?" Being able to admit to being wrong helps the learning process, and may open other doors. When I was in my clinical rotation at St. Louis University Medical School, I made a mistake. We were working at the State Hospital and I was number twelve on the rotation to get a new patient. We hadn't had a patient admitted all morning. I was feeling low and decided to run out and pick up my mail. When I got back the chief resident was looking for me. He was so angry at me; he kicked me off his service. I was called in to talk to the administrative staff. I told them directly what the circumstances had been, that I had made an error in judgment, and that I would not do it again. Because of that event, I became friends with the clinical head of the department, and he was one of the people I asked to write a reference for me to the psychiatric residency program I applied for. I never knew what he said about me, but when I went for my interview with Dr. Roy Grinker, the head of the Michael Reese Hospital residency program, the first words out of his mouth after he laid down the reports he was reading was, "Campbell, what is it about you that gets you such glowing references?"

Admitting ignorance ("I don't know') is necessary to learning. You have to agree to be taught if you want to learn quickly. Honesty about what you don't know is a good first step.

Being willing to run your own experiment is a great help. Learning is the exploration of uncharted territory. When you are learning you are moving into the unknown. See if the approach works for you. The more you know about something, the more you own it, and the less you fear it. Bringing an element of objectiveness to the situation will help you learn the choice approach more rapidly.

The more you understand that you create the vast majority of your life experiences, the more quickly you will learn you have the power to create specific experiences. Learning is more than just putting the information into your head. You have to assimilate the material and use it resourcefully.

Reading the material is planting the seed; putting it into practice is harvesting it.

To learn, you must have some basic trust. You need not blindly trust what others say, but you do have to suspend judgment and act as if you believe something is possible in order to give it a fair test (AA uses this concept: "Fake it until you make it").

Identify what benefits you might be getting out of being sick (sympathy, attention, control). If you can let go of these things you can make quicker progress.

The better you accept current reality, the faster you will see how unproductive your efforts are to change others, and how productive making different choices can be.

The more you take responsibility, and the better you understand assigned accountability the quicker you will learn.

If you can see and acknowledge the success in your life, you will grow faster than if you only look at your perceived deficits.

Most people over the age of 12 years have the ability to use the choice principles. Children below 12 years can make choices, but developmental factors (being in the blame system and not being able to get out of it until 12 years) have a significant influence on them and on the choices they see as available.

High moralistic or righteous beliefs often prevent resistant learners from finding new ways to deal with their problems. The more a person feels right about their beliefs the more they stay right where they are. I will sometimes tell patients if they need to leave my office with the same belief systems they came in with, I probably will not be able to help them.

Most people over twelve years old have developed cognitively to the point where they can use the choice principles presented in this book. In our resistant patient we find two characteristics: (1) They feel so righteous in believing others should change that their anger and resentment block their ability to learn; (2) They believe so completely that the world and others should change that they are unable to believe they can make choices that would lead to relief.

When asked, "How do you think you can best use these principles?" some people will say something like, "It depends on how my kids act this weekend." How well resistant learners use choice depends on how strongly they demand that the world around them has to change. If their demand for change in others is too strong, they simply will not learn how to use the choice system.

Children learn primarily from their experiences with the physical world; because of this they have very little understanding that the psychological world operates under a different set of principles.

If these principles still seem unclear, don't assume you are among those who cannot use the system. The choice system may be new to you. You may have to digest the method before you can use it in your life. The odds are, however, that you will have little difficulty understanding, or implementing, this approach on your own.

A formula some patients have found useful is ACT

1. Accept your current reality.
2. Choose to create through choice more of what you want in life.*
3. Take action; don't wait for others to create your experience.

> * Here is a place some people will get confused. It is important to understand that we are talking about choice of things that we can choose from. Every now and then a patient will say something to me like, "I can't just choose to be happy, you must be nuts" or "Well doc, if I can choose anything, I will just choose to be rich and happy." The confusion here is that there is a difference between choosing a product and choosing a means. I can choose to spend more time in acceptance, which will make the bottom line of happiness greater; I can not choose the product happiness. I can choose to get an

education or learn a special skill that will make the bottom line of wealth more of a reality; I can't just choose to be wealthy and have it appear.

Be precise in your language

Language is critical to the way we think. Many unspoken beliefs are buried in the words we use, and, unless you understand the concepts behind your words, you may end up making significant thinking errors. As you learn more about choice and change, you'll discover that each system has its own distinct language. The change system's language is derived from the physical world; it is frequently based on blame and trying to change events. The choice system's language is derived from the psychological world and is based on awareness, choice, and creating desired experiences.

The system you are in determines the meanings you give to a word. One meaning may make sense in the physical world, but it may mean the opposite in the psychological world. Love, can be used in a manipulative way ("If you loved me, you would …!" "I will change if you will love me." "I will love you if you will change"). Choosing to love unconditionally is expansive ("I love you as you are").

As you become aware of the differences between trying to change something versus creating a new experience for yourself, be aware of the language you use. When you say, "I'll help you," do you really mean "I'll help you, so you'll like me more?" When you love others, what does that mean to you? Do you need them to make you happy? Or does it mean you appreciate and accept them exactly as they are?

Be precise in your language so that you don't fool yourself with appearances. If you say, "I make him dinner every night, because I love him" when you really mean "I make him dinner every night, because I want something from him," you only fool yourself. As you raise your awareness of the nature of the two systems, raise your awareness of the language you use to discuss each system.

Use critical opportunities to increase your skill at making choices

You already know something about the benefits of choice and about the drawbacks of trying to change current reality. If you feel that someone, or something, is causing your distress (your wife left with another man; you were fired), be aware that how you react to a situation is your responsibility. You always have current reality to deal with (your wife is gone; you're unemployed), but you don't have to be at the emotional mercy of your situation. When you see that you create your own response to your current reality ("I sank into depression when my wife left"; "I was furious when I was fired"), you are free to use your thoughts and actions to help you create other experiences you may want. Recognize that you may have a delay in creating a new feeling because your feelings are made up of a psychological part (how you choose to look at a situation) and a physiological part. The physiological part consists of automatic body reactions and complex electrochemical impulses. Because you can only indirectly affect the physiological part, it may take awhile to create a new feeling. Typically, it takes a 10-50 min period.

The following are examples of how new experiences can be created:

> "I accept the reality that my wife left me and that I feel depressed about it."

> "I choose to create my vision of a happy, meaningful relationship with a woman who loves me."

> "I will take action by joining a singles group and pursuing my interests in clubs, rather than being alone; I will keep myself fit and healthy so that I feel good about myself; I will widen the friendships I already have with single women."

Or:

> "I accept the fact that I was unfairly fired from my job and that I am furious about it."

"I choose to create my vision of feeling good and having a job I love."

"I will take action by applying for similar positions in other companies, by looking into other types of jobs I might like to do, by seriously examining if I have other interests I might be able to turn into a career with more schooling, and by finding out about financial aid at schools that could help me broaden my skills."

The crux of the choice system is this: Despite the influences around you, you are responsible for how you choose to think, feel and act. The accountability for what happens to you is yours—as is the opportunity to create the life you want. Let go of the need to change yourself, other people, or events; you will be free of psychological pain. Nothing "out there" can dictate how you think, feel, and act. Each of those is entirely your choice. When you carefully begin to move these feelings into the proper category of cause and effect, or sequential ordering of events, you will find the causal list getting much smaller. In the remaining events you need to see if you can identify the accurate cause of your particular feeling.

An example of what I am not saying is this: If it is zero degrees outside and you take off all of your clothes and run outside, the experience will be to get cold. I am not suggesting that you can just tell yourself you are not cold and you will get rid of the feeling of cold. Maybe some Tibetan Monks can do that, but most of us can't. So how are we responsible for the cold feeling, and how can we get rid of it? Some of you will want to take the position that it is the cold temperature that caused the feeling of cold. But think about how long the cold had been there, and yet you did not feel cold. No, the cold did not cause your experience of being cold, it was one of the choices available to you; there were things you had to do to have that experience. In this example there were actually two things you did that opened you to the experience of cold. One: You took off your clothes. That in it's self may not have led to feeling cold. Two: You ran outside. Now you have created the proper conditions to experience cold. If you had put on clothes, you might have avoided feeling cold, even if action two followed. When we look carefully, we can usually see the roles we have in bringing events about; we are not always good at identifying them. Children in particular have a problem looking at their roles; they often feel they are being blamed for something when someone tries to talk to them about their role.

Understand the difference between cause and effect and sequential ordering of events

One of the problems adults have is that they continue to think and, often, to talk like children. Children put cause and effect interpretations on almost everything they experience. Immanuel Kant reportedly said that, "people are intrinsically configured to see cause and effect. It is just something the human race does." Children are able, cognitively, to understand the difference after the age of twelve. Like many things in life, however, if we do not think about it, we do not recognize it. We must begin to understand and use the difference in our thinking and our speech.

Be aware that the physical world and the psychological world work on different principles and have different languages associated with them.

An example is pain: in the physical world when things hurt us we try to move away from the cause, and we do the same when things are too loud, too sharp, too hard, and too scratchy. In the psychological world when we try to deal with psychological pain by getting away from it, we create more problems, and what we are attempting to create (no pain) is thwarted. In the psychological world we must confront things, we "must get in touch" with them in order for them to go away. This is completely opposite of the physical world. This is why therapists attempt to get people to "face their fears," "get in touch" with their feelings, and "embrace" their anxiety.

Other concepts that can also help to get rid of psychological pain

Letting go of psychological pain is possible

The common denominator in all emotional pain is need. Whenever people need self, situation, or others to be different from what they believe the situation to be, they go into psychological pain. The need can be specific

("I need my retarded child to be normal"; "I need a job"; I need my daughter to be off drugs"; "I need my husband to come back"), or general ("I need to change my whole life"). You stay in need and continue to try to change what is generally impossible to change; you keep trying and you keep hurting. You may learn to live with the pain ("It's my cross to bear"); you may try to numb it with drugs, alcohol, or work; you continue to hurt because you continue in need.

Need creates psychological pain

You can eliminate psychological pain by letting go of the need to change your current reality. When you use the choice system to accept current reality, you dissolve need, and your pain disappears. You should understand this does not always make the problem go away—just the pain.

I have seen hundreds of patients turn off their psychological pain once they accept current reality. Accepting current reality means honestly acknowledging what exists. You tell yourself the truth. You don't ignore what you dislike, exaggerate it negatively, or exaggerate it positively. You look at it in a clear and objective way. After you have a clear picture of what you have been rejecting, you consciously have to allow it to exist. Rather then fighting it, or forbidding it to be, you permit it to exist.

You include what you are resisting in your picture of current reality, rather than trying to exclude it. Acceptance is a perception ("This is how it is"), a decision ("I'll let it be"), and a feeling ("I'll experience it as it is."); it is neither "giving up" nor "resignation."

How feelings work

Your lack of acceptance creates negative emotions (feelings). Emotions (feelings) play a crucial role in human development. Your four basic emotions—mad, sad, glad and scared—can inspire you to action, nudge you to protect yourself, and urge you to cut your losses. The same cognitive event that creates feelings, also motivates us to take action, or avoid action. You do what you perceive <u>makes you</u> feel good, and you avoid what you believe <u>makes you</u> feel bad. After you take the action, your feelings leave, and so can your motivation.

The cognitive event that creates pleasure motivates you to move toward something. In some circles it is felt that emotions themselves create a given response. I do not adhere to that point of view. I believe emotions are the product of a cognitive process in the same way actions are a product of a cognitive process. Simply, because we are not aware word for word what that process is does not mean it is not occurring. To give feelings the attribute of intelligence makes no sense to me, whatsoever. It could be said there are actions that are not a product of thinking (cognition)—knee jerks for instance—but again, I would have a hard time putting intelligence on that action. Perhaps one could make a case for there being "knee jerk emotions." If that were so, it still would not meet my criteria for "intelligent" behavior. Intelligent emotions are like saying heat is intelligent or snow is intelligent. What feelings have in common with snow, or heat, is that they are all products.

When your cognitive balance sheet is pleasurable the experience motivates you to move toward something. The cognition that creates anxiety, motivates you to run, or escape, from a possible threat.

The cognition that creates anger motivates you to fight against a perceived threat. You yell, or you attack, someone to get rid of your perception that you are being slighted, abused or victimized, even though you know at some level your outburst will make matters worse. Parents ask why their child will lie, when the child knows they will be punished harder for doing that. The answer does not take four years on an analyst's couch. It is merely what the child's brain is telling them to do. If you say, "That is illogical," I would agree with you completely. It is only one of numerous examples of where the developing brain is totally illogical: one type of illogical pattern reaching into adulthood is blaming and another is the belief that emotions have intelligence.

The cognition that creates sadness motivates you to shut down and to withdraw after a loss. If you lose money in the stock market, the cognition that creates your sad feelings also motivates you to stop playing the market, and it has you act to protect the money you have left.

Normally your emotions will keep themselves in balance. Our emotions can be seen as part of a loop. Thoughts cause emotions or actions. In turn emotions and actions can influence our thinking in the same way the product snow or heat will influence the clothes I chose to wear. The products anxiety, fear, etc will influence our thinking and our actions. If you're scared long enough, you could eventually get mad and fight for your rights. If you're angry long enough, you may eventually fear the consequences of your anger and back off. If you are lucky in gambling, the pleasurable feeling you may have experienced (believing that the win made you happy), will work against the thoughts that it is dangerous behavior, and the odds are against you. When asked about Russian roulette, adolescents report believing a one out of six is good odds for surviving. Most well-developed adults will say that no odds are worth the possibility of killing themselves in such a needless manner.

Your need to change current reality, creates an excess of negative emotions. Too much sadness becomes depression, too much gladness becomes mania, too much fear becomes panic, and too much anger becomes rage. Your emotional thermostat malfunctions and you become emotionally distressed.

Your strong emotions (rage, panic, despair) may be part of a primitive survival system. They might help in times of real physical danger (a physical attack, or a fire), but in modern life this primitive motivational backup system (in which you automatically cement your psychological experiences to the physical world) is rarely needed. Using this feeling system as a guide is an unnecessary, ineffective, and generally irrational way to run your life. Daily, in my office, I see people ruin their relationships, because they are running with their emotions in situation after situation, rather than dealing with the cause of the emotions.

Choice, unlike the old, unsatisfactory change system which tries to balance the world, allows you to balance your emotions. When you use psychological principles (acceptance, movement, selection, and choice) to separate the physical world from your psychological world ("I accept the fact, I didn't get this job, and I choose to imagine a job I want"), you eliminate negative feelings. Your brain stops firing off distress signals, because you no longer need the world to be different. You create the experiences you want by using psychological principles, thereby, freeing yourself from the physiological messages.

Feelings can be perceived as a pressure on yourself. When you need to change the world, you use your unpleasant feelings as self-manipulation. You nudge, or goad, yourself to solve your problem. You make yourself anxious, so you won't forget all the work needing to be done. You get angry, so you'll stand up for yourself and set limits. You become depressed, so you can withdraw, regain your strength, and feel good again. (This is the base for the idea of intelligent emotions.)

Unfortunately, these approaches waste huge amounts of the limited energy resources you are drawing from. They will wear you out, and leave you stranded, like a car out of gas on the busy highway of life.

Emotional crisis management

You have two feedback mechanisms: your emotional and your goal-reaching mechanisms. The two often interact and influence each other. Your anxiety about a car accident can motivate you to use your seat belt. Using emotions to motivate your actions is often an automatic, unaware process.

You can, however, use your goal-reaching mechanism without any emotional input. For example, you could decide to use your seat belt simply because you decide to, or because it is the law, or because you understand it is safer.

You can use your feelings to pressure yourself, but you're nearly always better off using assessment and choice to create what you want. You don't have to put yourself through an emotional wringer when you use assessment and choice.

For example, when you stay in choice, fear is no excuse for being untrue to your vision: You just act. You accept the reality of your fear ("I'm afraid of being rejected"); choose and envision what you want (to go on a date); and take action to get it (make the phone call).

Feelings: how they use you

You are more, or less, at the mercy of what you refuse to accept, and what you resist captures your attention and enslaves you. Your focus becomes fixed on what you don't want. If you refuse to accept your feelings, they will push you around. We call to ourselves that which we say we want the least.

When you need to change current reality, your feelings begin to run your life ("I can't give speeches because I'm too anxious"; "I can't do my work because I'm too depressed"; I can't talk to them because I'm too angry"). What you want takes a back seat to your automatic reactions. Your feelings become excuses, or self-created handicaps ("I can't do anything until I feel better").

Big choices, little choices

You can't always feel the way you would like to feel at each moment. However, you do have the option to step over your feelings—your primitive motivational system—and move toward your vision. This is done by replacing the emotional engine with assessment and thought.

Moving off the Fence

Your feeling (the product of your thoughts) always takes you to the status quo. A person will withdraw from others when they feel threatened, and will move toward others when they feel lonely. Learning to be responsible for your choices, and not trying to be responsible for other's choices, help people get off the fence. It is equally important to stop making others responsible for your experiences, as it is to stop making yourself responsible for other's thoughts, feelings and actions.

Be cautious of the feeling that things have changed. Change, if you recall, is a physical world event, and it should be kept in that realm. When people begin to think they have changed, they think they have reached some level of consistency, or permanency, which is most likely inaccurate. I caution my patients in treatment for alcohol that the first indication they are on the way to a relapse is when they start saying something has changed.

Once we realize we create our own feelings, we no longer need to feel the vulnerability we had before. We can reframe our intentions to "want to" rather than "have to". This ability to reframe our feelings allows us to stabilize feelings; we are no longer easily blown off course. Because we gain an understanding that we can guide our feelings in a direction we desire, there is no reason to straddle the fence. If we don't like the side we came down on, we can make choices to get to the other side.

When you are in distress you erroneously believe your feelings will never change. This is one of the reasons people try to control the situation they are in. Struggling to change, or control, events, or feelings, only prolongs the unpleasant experience. Your feelings will naturally evolve as a new product (of your thinking); they will move toward the direction you want, if you focus on choice, instead of change.

Feelings: how to deal with them the way you want

Does being responsible for your feelings mean you can direct them at will and feel any way you want to? Your feelings are created by a complex biological and psychological feedback system. You often have little say over the onset of your spontaneous moods and feelings, which are physical phenomena.

Still, you have the responsibility for your feelings, because you are the one who can do the most about them. You have the responsibility, or choice, in how you interpret your feelings (their causes, meanings, and purposes). You have choice in how you express your feelings. You have the choice about how you manage your feelings (represses, feel, or ignore). You have the choice of directly affecting your feelings by which system of thinking you are operating in (change or choice system). Like a martial arts master, you can also learn to condition the mind to react in a particular manner, or way, to stimuli. And, importantly, you have the choice as to how you internalize your feelings (accept or reject them).

Some useful guidelines for dealing with your feelings:

Hold yourself accountable for your feelings ("I'm directly and indirectly responsible for my anger") rather than assigning the accountability (or blame) to others ("You <u>made me</u> mad").

Hold your vision despite what you're feeling at the moment ("I want this marriage to work, even though right now I feel its hopeless") rather than letting yourself be blown about by your feelings ("I feel so awful I don't even care what I want").

Express your feelings if it will help you reach your vision ("When you do that, I feel . . ."), rather than using your feelings to manipulate others ("Why do you do this to me?").

Express your feelings in a constructive way ("I feel bad when you're sarcastic*, and I'd like to resolve this somehow") rather than destructively ("You're sadistic!"). *Remember sarcasm, like beauty, is in the eye of the beholder, and the person you think is being sarcastic may not either intend, or see, what they are saying as sarcastic.

Experience your feeling ("I'll experience my feeling for forty-five seconds, and then I will focus on what needs to be done"), rather than repressing or changing your feelings ("I can't stand feeling like this").

Honestly acknowledge what you are feeling ("I'm feeling down at the moment") rather than denying or lying to yourself ("I don't feel bad").

Use choice to create the feelings you want ("I'll choose to have a good time") instead of trying to change others, or events, in order to feel good ("Why are they like this?").

Don't use your feelings to evaluate, or judge yourself. Just because you feel guilty doesn't mean you're a criminal; if you don't feel guilty, it doesn't mean you're not a criminal. Avoid evaluations of yourself, or others, when you are having strong feelings.

> Use the word FEEL as shorthand to remember these guidelines:
> Focus on your feelings.
> Express them constructively.
> Experience them.
> Let them go.

Acceptance: taking information in and letting pain go

In the physical world, when you take in, or accept, something, you're stuck with it until you sell it, give it away, or destroy it. In the psychological world, taking in (accepting) or rejecting information is the way you program the part of the mind that functions like a computer processor. If you do not accept what a friend is doing as helpful, you are essentially programming the brain to see them as hurtful, rather than helpful. If you accept, they are indeed a friend, you still may not choose to accept what they tell you as accurate for your needs, but it does not have the need to see them as an enemy. This is especially important in a period when people are so divided along political lines.

Acceptance is taking in wanted and unwanted information about current reality ("I think you really do care about me," or "I lost my job"). Once you have this information, you are better able to create what you want. How you take (accept) the information in is crucial to leading a happy and satisfied life. Do you take information in easily? Do you take it in poorly? Do you tell yourself "I can't take it in at all!"

The acceptor

The acceptor is a metaphor Gary Emery developed for the part of your brain that takes in information and either gives it the status of acceptance, or rejects it. Although the acceptor is not an actual, or physical, part of the brain, the metaphor seems to have found perceptual usefulness.

When the consciousness flow is blocked

You process a stream of consciousness about current reality through your acceptor. What you assess to be useful you keep, and what you believe isn't useful you attempt to discard. When you get a match between what you intend to have happen and what you see happening, you have motion toward your goal, and the emotional register is acceptance. However, when you have a mismatch, a clash between what you expect and what you see occurring, you experience lack of motion toward your goal and the emotional register is rejection. When the acceptance process turns out rejection, you experience emotional distress.

If you construct an image of current reality that is distorted ("Bill thinks I'm a fool"); you have a mismatch between what you need to have happen and your image of what is acceptable ("I need to have others' approval, but no one seems to like me"). Your emotional reaction to the rejected image blocks the flow of consciousness ("I feel bad").

How the acceptor gets blocked

Event: Mary didn't call. The perception of events is colored by past memories ("I've been rejected by her and others before"); an old perception surfaces ("Mary's rejecting me again). This belief is filtered through the interpretation department, and it is matched against other beliefs ("I need to be loved"). The mismatch between perception and belief blocks acceptance of Mary, or what Mary is doing, and creates negative feelings ("I'm feeling hurt and sad"). Your beliefs ("To be happy I need others to accept me") conflict with your image, or picture, of current reality. These beliefs are usually formed early in life; they are often generated by some trauma you didn't fully process in the literature; these are sometimes called "scripts".

Once you take in what you have been rejecting, you will often feel a physical release and your senses will become more acute—colors are brighter, sounds are clearer.

Smooth flow versus sluggishness

Some people have open acceptors; they easily process the daily demands of living, and if necessary, absorb major losses, such as the death of a mate, with little difficulty. The ups and downs of life flow smoothly through their acceptors.

Other people have sluggish acceptors. They often feel blocked ("I can't stand what's going on"), and even when their acceptors work, they accept only a trickle of current reality ("I can hardly put up with this"). The gap, or mismatch, between what they need and how they see current reality is large. They have more distorted images of reality ("Others will humiliate me") than people with open acceptors, and they react more strongly ("I need others' love"; "I need to be perfect"; "I need to be in control"; "I can't trust others"; "I don't belong"; "I can't do it").

Overly reactive people have trouble accepting even simple events in their lives (that everyone does not love them, or mother may not want to return their call). They jerk through life rather than flow through it. When their assessments of events differ from their desire, their acceptor jams up, and they have trouble processing the life experiences.

How you take in and process current reality is often related to early learning experiences. If, as a child, you had severe trauma (a psychotic mother, for example), you may have trouble accepting later losses. You may have developed a belief that you can't stand losses, or setbacks. It is as if your acceptor, after having to expand too much as a child, has since collapsed and narrowed. Similarly, if you were overprotected as a child, you'll likely have trouble with acceptance. You may expect everything to go well, and because of under use your acceptor may fail to develop fully; you then have difficulty processing unpleasant experiences. If you observe little children, they are a whirlwind of acceptance and rejection in process.

Too much too soon

Even if you're good at accepting adversity, you may have trouble if too much happens all at once. An accumulation of big and small setbacks can block your acceptor. Once you start resisting reality, you have trouble accepting anything: the way you look, the way your wife talks, or how your kids act.

Generally, acceptance goes unnoticed; you process experiences in an even flow until there is a conflict. Then you experience pain, and it is as if you put in some debris that blocks your acceptor. As with your digestive system, you only notice your acceptor when something is wrong.

Signs of Blockage

Once your acceptor is blocked, you're not interested in anything but the problem. Because you spend your energy fighting current reality, you may be chronically fatigued and "stressed out." You may cry all the time or you may be unable to cry. You may feel compelled to talk about the problem, or you may not be able to talk about it at all. Excesses in sleeping, drinking, and working are attempts to deal with your resistance to current reality.

The view

When you resist current reality, you constrict your awareness of available choices. The conscious portion of your brain (left hemisphere) fills up with racing, obsessive thoughts and you become fixated on what you want to change. You go into a trancelike state and react to the image, as if it were true.

In his book *The War Against Sleep*, Colin Wilson, an influential writer about split-brain research, calls the left hemisphere pessimistic because it looks too closely at life—like trying to decide on the worth of the Mona Lisa by examining the canvas with a magnifying glass, or microscope.

In short, the view from the left-brain is negative by nature. The view from the right brain is positive by nature, revealing vistas of meaning and an interconnectedness that is not readily conscious.

You have many thinking distortions when you're upset, because you lack perspective; you're looking too closely at the problem and missing the big picture. Our view has an evolutionary purpose. If I see danger in too many places, I am more likely to survive than if I see danger in too few places. If our ancestors had ignored, or overlooked, what was dangerous—a tiger, for example, or possible starvation—we would not be here.

When you resist something, it's similar to walking around with your hand in front of your face. Notice the difference in your range of awareness and your options when you either resist current reality, or when you accept it. To get rapid relief, you need to use psychological principles of choice, selection, movement; the physical principles of change or control are nearly always counterproductive because they reduce awareness and options.

What you see is what you get. Mother Nature seems to send us what we dislike the most. If you can't stand dirt; you see dirt everywhere. What you fear is sure to come visiting at your doorstep. If you try to block out what you don't want to hear, you can't help but hear it. Have you ever known people who hate being fat, or hate being sick, or hate being angry? Their problems seem to cling to them, because they concentrate on them so fully that they shut out other, good things.

When a patient says, "I can stand anything but this one area" (rejection, disloyalty, failure), that is what the therapy is going to be about. The more an individual needs to change something, the more it tends to stay the same. It also becomes the way other will then blackmail them to get what they want.

In the choice system, you can use the psychological principle "what you see is what you get" to your advantage: You hold the vision of what you want until you get it. The trick is to focus on what you want until it happens. By holding the vision, you increase your awareness of what specific actions to take to create it.

Needing to change your need to change

When you realize that you have been trying to change reality, be on the lookout for your attempts to change that orientation. You may try to use your willpower to do this ("I've got to change my thinking"), or you can force yourself to think about something else ("I'm not going to think about trying to change my husband"). However, these methods seldom work; they're the same methods that created your distress. Even if you can repress, or bury an experience, it always returns. Someone mentions your old boyfriend, or girlfriend, and you feel like crying. The unaccepted memory, or repressed behavior, rises up like a hand from the grave to grab you.

Facing the feeling

You have to start by accepting your resistance. What you resist most are your feelings; they often seem like monsters. This is especially true if you see them as causes, rather than products, of your thinking. Acting out your lack of acceptance, through avoiding what '<u>makes you</u>' feel bad ("I can't tell him the truth"; "I can't talk in public"), influences the production of your anxiety. When you avoid something (public speaking), you reinforce the illusion that the event (the speech), or others (the audience), have the ability to '<u>make you</u>' feel bad. Moving toward what is frightening ("I'll ask her out"), or uncomfortable ("I'll try even though I'm unsure"), causes the discomfort to disappear.

Avoidance has a cumulative effect ("I'll avoid all men because they can hurt me"), and it causes life to become increasingly difficult and barren ("Is this all there is?"). Approaching what you fear is effective, because you accept and acknowledge current reality, and you thus free creative energy.

Acceptance keeps you current. Everything you refuse to accept in your past robs you of living fully in the present. If there is something that happened to you last week that you can't accept, then you're not taking in and enjoying what is happening right now. If you have a large backlog of unprocessed experiences, you will have a strong sense of missing out on life, and you will have a greater fear of dying.

Once you tell yourself the truth about current reality ("I'm fifty-five years old, have a stressful job, and eat and smoke too much; this <u>makes me</u> a candidate for a heart attack"), you can create what you want ("I'll check myself out with the doctor, and I will get myself healthy"). You develop the clarity and energy to move beyond your current obstacle, and you create what you want.

Becoming wiser

When you are in the flow, you take what is useful (the nutrients) from current reality and eliminate the rest. If your acceptor leaks like a sieve, you fail to learn from your experiences. You keep making the same mistakes.

INFLUENCES ON YOUR ACCEPTOR

Biological influences

When your biological system is "off center," accept this as current reality. At times you may have to put off processing, or accepting, a troublesome situation until you are feeling physically stronger. You need a certain amount of psychological energy to run your psychological world effectively. Anything that depletes this energy (anger, envy, greed, fear, a physical ailment, alcohol, drugs) makes acceptance more difficult. When your energy level is down, your acceptor works less effectively. You're less able to accept current reality when you're sick, tired, hungry, excited, or stressed.

Social influences

When you start creating your own life, you stop being bullied by cultural imperatives. For example, if you are the only one of a large family to remain single and your family pressures you to get married, you can accept the situation by taking responsibility for your own choices ("I'm the only one who can put psychological pressure on me").

Until you hold only yourself accountable for your choices, you'll have trouble accepting something if you're the only one with the "problem." If what you have to accept goes against group norms, if the group puts up psychological barriers to your accepting it, or if you may lose social status for doing so, you may have problems with acceptance.

Psychological influences

Being for acceptance makes your acceptor flow. A psychological bias against acceptance undermines the ability to accept. If you're against something, you set up barriers to it. For example, if you're a negative person ("No, no, no!"), you will have problems accepting current reality.

Your bias may be due to misconceptions about acceptance. The most common misconception confuses physical meanings of acceptance (resignation, giving up, settling for, losing control, being weak) with the psychological meaning of acceptance (an honest look at current reality for the expressed purpose of grounding yourself in current reality and creating what you want). Acceptance is the first step you take, not the last.

Taking that first step

Some experiences are more difficult to accept than others. You may have to begin by accepting only a small part of an experience, or by accepting it for a few moments at a time. No matter how overwhelming current reality may seem, you can accept it. Once you accept reality, you set the stage for feeling better.

Like attracts like

Acceptance creates peak experiences. We are all interdependent, and we live in one world in one universe. There is a natural progression to this realization. First, when your acceptor is working you accept yourself ("I accept the way I look"; "I love my gray hair"). When you like yourself, you are free to be yourself. Second, you like what is like yourself ("I like him; he has an irreverent sense of humor, like me"; "I like this house; it has character"). When you accept others, you begin to see how similar they are to you, and you start to like them. And, third, if you can accept the differences between you and others, you move to a higher state. The feeling of connectedness with others leads to a larger cosmic sense of oneself.

The decision to accept other people as they are saves many family relationships. It is one of the most difficult acceptance tasks I experience people struggling with in my office. In a typical family situation, the parents are adamantly against drugs; their teenaged children choose to take drugs, and they make this their battleground with the parents. When parents are able to accept (grounding in current reality) the fact that their child may use drugs despite their wishes; proceed with setting limits they can enforce; they keep the relationship alive, and there is often a major improvement in the relationship.

Rather than feeling helpless, frustrated, and hopeless, the parents should realize that they do have effective responses they can make. They cannot make a child decide not to use drugs (a decision for which only the child has responsibility), but they can hold the child accountable. For example, they can tie drug, or alcohol, use to the use of the car; they can make less money available; they can refuse to provide laundry facilities as long as the child is using drugs. They can let the child know they will not tolerate the behavior. They can make it clear that if they discover drug use in the house, they will turn the child in to the police; that if they know the child is at a party where the drugs are available, they will call the police; and if they find out who provides the drugs, they will call the providers and let them know that selling to their child will put the seller at risk of being turned in to the police.

This process clarifies responsibilities. The child can make the choice to take drugs. The parents accept that, but let the child know that they have responses/choices they can and will make. Once the limits are set, the child has to pay the cost of taking drugs (no money, no car, less freedom). Often, as the cost goes up, the child decides to give up using drugs. The current political experiment of not holding people responsible for their acts has resulted in far more of the same acts. This would be expected by people who actually give consideration to the outcome of their actions.

When you accept something, you've been resisting you may feel an immediate, acute sadness, then experience a release of painful feeling. When your stream of consciousness starts flowing again, you are happy and more at one with the world. Acceptance removes the barrier between you and the world.

Acceptance strategies

When General George Patton wanted something done, he told his officers exactly what he wanted, and then he left the "how" up to them. He said their creativity and the effective ways they accomplished the goals, when left to their own devices, often surprised him.

In the choice system, the "how" question is always primary. Einstein once said something like "True intelligence is not determined as much by the answers people give, as it is by the questions they ask." In the choice system the basic assumption is that we create our own experience. If I am creating my experience, the next most important thing for me to determine is how am I creating the experience I am having? Teenagers and young adults have a great deal of trouble here. When others attempt to get them to look at what they have created, and to understand the mechanism that brought it about, they have a tendency not to listen. The problem is that they do not understand the importance and necessity of examining their role in what has just happened. They do not make accurate associations about the choices and the products that have been created by those choices. They misunderstand the role they, and others, have had in this creation process. They believe when people are trying to help them understand their role in events that they are being criticized, or are being held to blame. Both of these mental positions prevent acceptance of what they are being taught. Once a person understands a cause-and-effect relationship where it actually exists (i.e., blaming causes anger), they have a mechanism to prevent the product (anger goes away when you stop blaming). What you want is to build a warehouse of understanding.

As there are *"Fifty Ways to Leave Your Lover,"* according to the song, there are more than fifty ways to reach acceptance. You may already have your own personal acceptance strategies, or you may be a person who enjoys making them up as you go along. Pick strategies that appeal to you and experiment until you find what works best for you. You may find that a strategy that works one time may not work at another, so make sure you have more than one strategy in your pocket. Agility comes with practice.

The ways to accept current reality are broken down here into awareness strategies, feeling strategies, thinking strategies, and acting strategies.

Awareness strategies

Attempts to deny, ignore, and rationalize away reality are major obstacles to acceptance; therefore, they are obstacles to pleasure in life. Acceptance and awareness are directly related, if you increase one, you increase the other. You can use many different ways to increase your awareness of current reality. Different individuals find different ways more, or less, useful. Stick with those that help you.

Observe yourself

You become better at acceptance the more you know how it works. Looking objectively at yourself, as if you were another person, is often a help to get a better understanding of how you approach problems and work things through.

Know what you want

Accepting current reality is easier if you have a vision of what you want. Often you are so busy resisting that you never get around to deciding what you do want. Remember that in the creative process acceptance is not the final step, but it is the initial step in creating the experiences you want. There is an ancient saying, "If you don't know where you want to go, you will not recognize it when you get there."

Define what you want

A simple and easy way to resolve a conflict is to move on to something better. You increase your acceptance when you define what that "something better" is for you. Acceptance does not always mean that we must resolve something right now. Time actually takes care of a lot of things. Acceptance might mean being willing to wait and see where nature is going to lead us. I encourage my patients to accept that there is usually plenty of time for them to be upset after something happens. They don't need to get an early start on it.

Focus in on the experience you want

If you find that what you want is impossible, focus on the general psychological experience you want, not on a specific goal.

PATIENT: "I want Sue to come back, and have her love me again." (The specific goal)

THERAPIST: "For what reason?"

PATIENT: "So I'll be happy again." (More general experience)

THERAPIST: "Anything else?"

PATIENT: "I want to be in a good relationship." (More general experience)

THERAPIST: "Okay, what you want is to be happy and to be in a good love relationship. Sue is only one option, and she may not be the option available for creating what you want."

What if you don't know what you want? Robert Fritz, the founder of DMA (a course that teaches creativity), has given a profound answer to this question: "You make it up." Simply make up a vision of what you want, and if, after you get it, it turns out you don't like it, make up another one. Be specific about what you make up because clarity equals success. The more specific you are in your vision ("I want to be in my own one-bedroom condo near the beach"), the easier your vision will be to create.

In the physical world objects exist whether you think about them, or not, and despite what you think of them. In your psychological world nothing exists for you until you create it mentally. If you want a vision you consider worthy of you, you need to make it up; its existence is entirely dependent upon you.

In the psychological world you also make up how you achieve your vision. Suppose you want to go back to school. You make up what you want to study ("computers") and you make up how you accomplish it ("I'll go to night school").

Rediscover old strategies

You may not realize it, but you have been able to accept many past ordeals. You already have a set of skills you can use, even though you may not be aware of them.

What works for you may not work for someone else, and vice versa.

Go with the flow

You can reach acceptance by imitating nature. Nature is powerful because nature accepts all—birth, death, and everything in between. Nature delights in acceptance. The river accepts whatever is in its way, and moves on. If necessary, the river will go around mountains or under them. Nature is unconcerned with good or bad; it just keeps accepting and moving on.

Writer May Saxton has captured this spirit: "I think of the trees and how simply they let go, let fall the riches of a season, how without grief (it seems) they can let go and go deep into their roots for renewal and sleep."

When you accept, you flow with Mother Nature. If your boss at work is a tyrant, that's the way Mother Nature designed it. Given your boss's genetic, social, and psychological background, your boss is likely to be the way he or she, is at the moment because of those factors. Dr. Richard Feynman, a California Institute of Technology physicist and Nobel laureate, has said, "Don't keep saying to yourself, 'How can it be like that?' because you will go into a blind alley nobody has yet escaped from. Nobody knows how it can be like that." Mother Nature is the way she is. By collaborating with her, rather than fighting with her, you can get more of what you want.

Contemplate acceptance

Think about how you can be more accepting during the day. The more you reflect on acceptance, the better you are at putting it into practice. For example, you might meditate in the morning on accepting difficulties you foresee later in the day (an unpleasant meeting, hassles getting to work, having to get through some work you've been avoiding).

I once had an opportunity to purchase a Jaguar XKE. It was a wonderful car. It had a characteristic I was warned about (by one of my patients) before I bought it. It was always breaking down. I chose to accept that aspect of the car, and I enjoyed it for many years even though it was in the shop about as much as it was out. Then, I decided I no longer wanted that experience, and I got rid of the car. To enjoy the car I had to accept its poor maintenance record. Fortunately, because I was warned about it ahead of time, I was able to make a decision before the purchase.

Read the classics

Acceptance is the theme of many classic books, such as the works of the Greek Stoics, Marcus Aurelius's *Meditations*, and the teaching stories of Saint Francis of Assisi. Acceptance is old wine in new bottles. You can learn the intellectual side of acceptance from reading the classics, but then go out and actually practice it. At first the intellectual side may be easiest to grasp. If you keep going back and forth between the intellectual and experiential, however, you will eventually need less reflection, and will be ready to accept current reality immediately.

See the good

You'll have an easier time with acceptance if you have a good word for every occasion. A clue: If people avoid you, your negativity may be the reason. People dislike being around someone who constantly devalues the world ("How was your visit to California?" ... "I hate Los Angeles; the smog's terrible and the people are shallow!"). Many adults avoid the company of adolescents, because they so often are contemptuous of everything.

You can easily get caught in a vicious cycle. First, you feel bad, because you believe you don't measure up to others. Then you try to feel better by putting others down. However, when you attempt to make yourself more, by making others less, the effort always backfires. You lessen yourself by being contemptuous and you end up feeling worse. You are usually a part of what you are putting down ("I despise the whole human species"). Notice how you describe life ("My car's a wreck, I live in a dump, and my wife is a mess").

What you give out is generally what you will get back. If you label others positively, you will be more inclined to label yourself positively. Mislabeling can be costly. If someone put skull and crossbones and wrote "Poison" on a container of helpful medicine, you probably wouldn't use that medicine, even though it could make you healthy. You want to label yourself and others in a way that is the most useful and truthful; labeling is a way of carrying things around on your shoulder, so, even better, don't label at all.

There is a story about a couple looking for a new home. They stop and ask an old man sitting on his porch what type of people live in the community. The old man asked "What kind of people lived where you came from? "They were mean and hard to get along with" was the reply. "That is the same type of people we have here," said the old man. Later another couple came by with the same question. This time their response to the old man was, "It was a great community, people were friendly and very helpful" and the old man's response was the same, "That is the same type of people we have here." We are likely to bring our perceptions along with us—so be careful how you see things.

Imitate the best in others

You will accept reality better if you had good coping models in the past (important people in your life who could accept their losses successfully). If your models used denial, projection, scapegoating, and rationalization, you'll probably have trouble with acceptance. Understanding this relationship can be helpful in getting out of the imitation trap.

Learn from your experience

If you look at current reality from a learning perspective ("Next time I'll do it differently") rather than a blaming perspective ("I've got to discover who's to blame"), you make the reality more acceptable. Blaming hampers acceptance. When you learn from current reality, you extract the ingredients that benefit you and expand your awareness. Ask yourself "What can I learn or take away from this?"

Some people suggest that suffering is good for us. This thinking is based on the observation that people are often wiser, more compassionate, and better people after they have gone through a trauma, or ordeal. But we need to understand that the suffering didn't make them better. The acceptance of their reality is the reason for their growth: their awareness has been expanded. You don't need to suffer to grow; you only need to accept more reality. Higher inflation, or a higher price for gas is only good for people if you want them to experience having less or doing less.

Get the facts

Acceptance requires fully acknowledging current reality. Get the facts, and you can increase your acceptance. Acquiring data helps in all forms of emotional distress. Once you know something, you can stop being overly impressed by it; you may stop fearing it.

You can learn to face the facts

By choosing to review an event, you actively counteract avoidance. With each review you see your situation in a larger and clearer context. As you move from the close up to wide-angle view, you correct distortions, and you make current reality easier to take.

Be honest with yourself and others

The best awareness strategy is to look at current reality as it is. Trim off excess baggage. Don't make it worse (or better) than it is. Look realistically and honestly at what you must accept.

Expand your viewpoint

Don't be fooled by the appearance of current reality. Wisdom knows the difference between the container and the contents. What you believe is too terrible to accept is often just the container (or appearance); when you get behind the appearance, you may find a blessing. Withhold judgment until you see the situation in its larger context. Tell yourself that you won't jump to conclusions until all of the facts are in.

Often, our awareness about the present lies in the future. You may not know until tomorrow, what the reason was for what happened today. This is why historians are constantly writing history books about past events. With time we can actually get a better perspective about events than we had when we were close to the event. However, by paying attention to current reality (the now), you expand your awareness, and you increase your ability to create a better future.

Feeling strategies

Your life experiences consist of thoughts, feelings/sensations and actions. If you're afraid of making a fool of yourself, what you're really afraid of are the cognitive products: shame, anxiety, and self-consciousness. If you're afraid of dying in an accident, you're likely afraid of the anticipated sensations of pain and panic or the negative and uncomfortable feeling of helplessness.

Remember, feelings are products of cognition, but they become feedback influencing cognition and action. The brain gives you a jolt to get your attention. As long as you resist or ignore emotional signals, the brain will continue to send them; once you accept the signals, the brain stops sending them.

Experience your feelings

The way out of your bad feelings is through them. You have to allow yourself to experience bad feelings to stop feeling bad. Once you get the hang of the process, it becomes incredibly simple to lessen your painful feelings. The concept "getting in touch" with your feelings is equivalent to clarifying your thinking or understanding the intent of your actions.

Welcome your feelings

Rapid shifts are not unusual. Once people learn to use acceptance, they can create different feelings almost immediately. This sometimes confuses other people who think rigidly, or who believe that you have to feel a certain way about events. In the hospitals where I worked, nurses used to complain to me that my patients got better too quickly. They had a rigid way of looking at things, and because of that perspective, they could not see how a person could make a rapid shift to a different way of feeling about a given situation. This is one of the ways, unfortunately and unintentionally, well meaning people actually contribute to others staying ill for a longer time.

Express your feelings

You may find it helpful to identify and then express your feelings out loud ("I'm feeling scared"), especially if you usually repress or ignore your feelings.

Your feelings move in stages along an emotional scale. If you're apathetic and down about a project, you usually have to go through fear, anger, and boredom before you get positive.

Other expressive behaviors, such as demonstrating anger by throwing balloons (or rolled up socks) with all your might at the wall, can be helpful. However, a potential problem with all expressive behaviors is that in carrying them out you can stimulate yourself and actually end up feeling worse.

Let yourself experience feelings of ambiguity. Life is a continual process of facing the unknown. We all live in a world of unknowns. Every moment is in some way new and unknown.

Focusing on the uniqueness of each moment is a powerful acceptance strategy. Let Nature have time to unfold. If you resist the ambiguity of the moment ("I need to know"), you're going to create more ambiguity. All you can count on are probabilities (most cars stop at red lights). The greater your ability to tolerate and love uncertainty, the happier and more successful you will be.

People usually react to the ambiguous situation in three ways:

- By seeking the answer to one arbitrary but unanswerable question ("How long will it take?"). The solution is to ask a better question ("How can I best accept the unknown?") rather than asking a question that has no answer.
- By jumping to a conclusion ("I know it'll turn out badly"). The solution is to expect the unexpected and tolerate the ambiguity and the fact that you can't know things for certain.
- By seeking constant validation that your answer is right ("I'll be okay, right?"). The solution is to experience your ambiguity and let go of your need for guarantees and constant reassurance.

Learning to accept the unknown is especially important when you're experiencing emotional distress. Your negative or fearful feelings and thoughts will cause you to jump to negative or fearful conclusions. When you're feeling calm, your hunches or intuitions are often right; emotional distress, on the other hand, shuts down your intuition, so your emotionally based hunches, or flashes of apparent intuition, are more frequently wrong. For example, many, if not most, people who take an airplane trip have automatic flashes of feeling that their plane might crash. But they realize that their premonitions are unfounded, so they fly anyway.

You can increase your tolerance for uncertainty with ambiguity training: accept past losses. If you accept unresolved past losses (such as the death of a parent), you'll have an easier time accepting current reality. Unresolved past losses hinder your acceptance of current reality, because they are a reminder that there is something you haven't accepted. You begin to think that maybe you don't have "acceptance ability," or that you don't have the ability to accept what is happening to you in the present. Consequently, you are at increased risk for depression.

Accept chains of feelings

What you resist usually comes in clusters. Think of all the things Katrina victims had to accept in only a few moments. Every day you'll have many opportunities to accept discomfort.

Flood yourself with the negative experience

Think about what you are rejecting; flood yourself with images and feelings of what you are fighting. There is a form of therapy used for phobias that is called "flooding." In this form of therapy, a person who is afraid of mice might be placed in a room filled with hundreds of mice. In a short time, the fear of mice will generally disappear. People who fear riding an elevator might get on an elevator and ride it for a full day. Again, the fear will generally disappear when this is done. There is an old saying, if you get bucked off a horse, you need to get right back on, or you may never ride again. Getting back on is a form of flooding ourselves with the negative experience.

Love the feeling

What can you love about the situation? Here is an opportunity to use the division strategy. See if you can love one percent of the situation. Look for something useful in it (there is always something), and love that. Is the experience a way to become wiser? Can it become a good anti-shame exercise? Is it a way to eliminate false pride? A former prisoner of war said he was able to stand the torture of his imprisonment by learning to love the pain. Mystics have written, "Hell loved is heaven." When you love your enemies, they don't stand a chance. Acceptance comes when we decide to love the experience we have. Love can solve nearly any problem, because it moves you up to a higher psychological level of functioning; love is thus a powerful acceptance strategy.

Take the opposite tact

Hate what you cannot accept. Exaggerate your need to change your feelings. Go way beyond your normal resistance. Forbid yourself to accept the situation ("I'll never accept this no matter what"). This strategy sometimes works because the mind is like a child and often does the opposite of what you tell it to do. Exaggeration is the key here.

Laugh at your painful experience

Many people use humor to accept adversity. When I can get someone in my office to exaggerate their fears to the point of ridiculousness, and when they start to laugh about what they were telling me, the fear quality generally reduces or disappears. I have seen laughter break suicidal individuals out of their morose attitude.

Be kind to yourself

People are rarely kind to themselves. When you are more self-compassionate and less self-contemptuous, you can accept adversity with more agility. Frequently, what you need to accept in order to get relief from emotional distress is yourself. A major psychological principle is "like begets like." When you treat someone with love, you start to love him, or her. Self-acceptance is similar, treat yourself as you would like others treat you.

Thinking and acting strategies

By thinking and acting in new ways, you can accept current reality. You can use many different methods to reach the same end. Hold onto your vision of acceptance of current reality and use what works for you.

Thinking strategies

We humans despair more than any other living creatures primarily because we can make ourselves unhappy. On the other hand, what makes us rather unique is our ability to direct and correct our thinking. When your thinking is straight and clear, you understand and accept reality better.

Your thoughts include choices in how you see reality ("This is good") and in how you act ("I'll go for it"). You can substitute or select a new thought to replace an old one. Substituting a new thought does not necessarily change the essence of the prior thought. Think of a circle. Now think of a triangle. Your thoughts of what constitutes a circle didn't change. In this book the opposite may occur. With each section that you read, what you thought you understood in the previous section may undergo a transformation. At times we must arrive at a new concept in increments. Think about how you learned to do division.

Thoughts create experiences/feelings

For example, the thought "I need to be perfect" may create the experience of, or product of, anxiety, internal pressure, frustration, a sense of failure or satisfaction, pride, or superiority. While you can't change this thought, you can select a different thought ("I'll accept any imperfections," "I will not go overboard with my successes"), and this will create a different experience. It is my estimate that 60% of our experiences occur between our ears. The rest is created by what exists around us.

Self-accountability—holding yourself answerable for all of your experiences—leads to greater awareness and acceptance, and thus to relief from pain and distress. Self-accountability is the opposite of blaming or making excuses.

Use the ACT formula

Suppose you want to lose weight, but you overeat at a party. You did this for one of several reasons: You may have had a feeling of free will, and you chose to overeat regardless of the consequences; or you didn't have a feeling of free will, and you just automatically, mindlessly, overate. You had conflict between your desire to feel better and your vision to be thin.

Usually, in such situations you don't have a feeling of free will; you go into a mild trace. Your awareness shrinks to the demands of the moment, and you lose your original vision. When that happens, you also lose your awareness;

you unconsciously eat. By getting down on yourself, you keep the trance going. Blaming yourself ("Why am I blimping out?") stops the process of acceptance, and it keeps you tranced out. You keep eating to try and feel better. You did what you did because at the time it seemed like a good idea. Given your level of constricted awareness, it was what you chose to do. A basic principle of psychology is, "People do the best they can given their current level of awareness." When you find yourself in the vicious circle of trance and blame, use the ACT Formula as soon as you can:

> Accept current reality.
> Create where you choose to go.
> Take action to get there.

Practice tolerance

Intolerance ("All Arabs are evil"; "Baseball is stupid") prevents acceptance. Belittling anything or anyone (your wife, kids, parents, job, house, car, town, and country) belittles you. You end up with less self-acceptance. You can use this rebound effect to your advantage. Accept others, and you'll accept yourself better.

Not forgiving is based on a need to change the past, and it occurs when you blame others for your experiences. When you run your life by choice, you give the experience to whomever it belongs ("My mother chose to criticize my competence: it's a free country; I have the choice to develop competency in any area I want").

Look for the grudge in what you have trouble accepting ("I can't forgive my ex-wife for leaving me for another man"). Pinpoint how you use blame in the grudge situation; then revisit the situation from a choice perspective ("My ex-wife did what she did; period; I can choose to feel angry about it or let it go"). When you don't forgive, you vote to keep your pain.

Value acceptance

Often, all you need in order to achieve acceptance is a desire. Start by raising your opinion of acceptance. Find ways to value and esteem it.

In other words, sell yourself on acceptance. Because a major block to acceptance is a need to change current reality, the phrase "Can I let go of the need to change this?" is to the point.

Develop a grace factor

In her book *Success Is the Quality of your Journey*, Jennifer James, a keen observer of life, suggests that you develop a 10 percent grace factor in your life. Assume that you'll get cheated about 10 percent of the time, that people will be rude 10 percent of the time, that you'll pay 10 percent more than your share that you'll lose about 10 percent of your belongings. With some people (your in-laws, your boss) and some places (foreign countries) you may need to have a 20 percent grace factor.

Develop a quota system

Ethnomethodologists (anthropologists who study ordinary life) have found that life for just about everyone in America can be put into one sentence: Life is one damn thing after another. The human brain is designed to find and solve problems. When one problem is solved, we find another one. Accept the reality that life is a series of obstacles or challenges.

Some of your difficulties are almost "laws of the universe." If you drive a car, the law of the universe says that you're going to have car trouble at times. If you have a dog, you will have dog piles to clean up. People enjoy Murphy's "laws" because they contain kernels of truth. You might write in your notebook, "Life is one damn thing after another," and refer back to it from time to time.

Appreciate half a loaf

Letting go of your demands for perfection will help you move toward acceptance. You'll stop feeling chronically let down. Revise your absolute standards ("My wife must always be cheerful, efficient, intelligent, and beautiful"). Let go of excess baggage and give up your perfectionism. You may be afraid if you let it go you'll be settling for the mediocre, but the paradox is that when you let perfectionism go you achieve more.

In the choice system you can be true to your visions, which are often high. You can hold on to your standards and honestly admit it when you fall short of them. However, unlike the perfectionist, you don't have to have a perfect physical world to be happy, and you can appreciate what you do have.

Serve your vision, not your perfectionism. Keeping your eye on what you want gives you energy. Focusing on flaws and mistakes depletes your energy. When you design your own life, you can appreciate and enjoy the present because you're moving toward what you love.

Adopt a mature attitude

Young children actively resist what they dislike. They are often in the change system (Mommy, I can't color inside the lines because you won't color with me"). An average adult may act like a baby once or twice a day, a small child 10 or fifteen times a day. Recall events of the last day or two. How many times did you "go baby"? (Damn it, my pencil broke;" "If I can't have the last piece of cake, I'm going to bed").

Imagine yourself in the same situation responding as a mature adult. When you have trouble accepting something, ask yourself, "What is the most mature way to handle this?"

Be flexible

Physical reality is constantly changing: If you accept this rather than fight it, you'll save yourself pain and the possibility of being left behind. Industrial psychologists have found that it is not change itself that workers resent and resist, but they resent not having a say in initiating the changes. No matter how the change is introduced to you, you must always initiate your own responses to it.

Stop with the why

The best way to resist current reality is to ask yourself, "Why? Why did it happen? Why Me?" Why means "I refuse to accept this." Why elicits thinking that raises unanswerable questions. To accept a situation, you have to stop asking why all the time.

Replace the why with why not. (For, "Why did this accident have to happen to me?" substitute, "Why not? It did happen to me") Why is another way of saying, "This shouldn't have happened." You fight with reality and bring yourself down. Why not on the other hand, allows you to collaborate with reality.

Another strategy for achieving acceptance is to replace the destructive why with the constructive where, or what. ("Where am I right now, and what do I want? I got a D on the test, and I want to get at least a B for the course"). "Why" questions keep you stuck. "Where" and "what" questions make you focus on current reality and on your vision.

Action strategies: be a doer

Alfred North Whitehead, considered the greatest Western philosopher since Plato, said, "We do not think first and act afterwards; from the moment of birth, we are immersed in action, and can only fitfully guide it by taking thought." In the final analysis, to the external world it's not what you think, or feel, that counts, but what you do. Be a doer and keep moving toward your visions.

There is a story about Bertram Russell being asked to give a graduation commencement address. After a lengthy introduction Mr. Russell walked to the podium and asked, "Who here wants to be a writer?" Hands went up all over the auditorium. "Then you should go home and start writing," he said, and he sat down.

Jump in, go around, or go over the obstacle in front of you: Make the phone call to clear up the department store bill, tell your boss you want a raise, and make an appointment with the doctor about your lump. Even a false start is usually better than no start. When you just think about a problem you stand still. Once you take action, you move vertically allowing you to gain a better view, and you can see, or open up, new paths of action.

Realign yourself

Line up your images (thoughts), feelings, and actions and move them in concert toward the goal (Internal consistency). When one of the three is out of line (internal inconsistency), focus on the other two ("I feel bad, but I'll choose to maintain a positive image and to act in a way that will contribute to feeling good"). Because emotional distress is a feeling (product), in order to create a new feeling, you often need first to focus on creating an image you want, and then acting in a way that is consistent to obtain the goal. To do this, act as if you accept current reality; be a psychological chiropractor and realign your actions and feelings.

Ask yourself what needs to be done behaviorally to reach acceptance—then do it. Try new activities. If you don't know something, admit it.

Make yourself decide

Often you resist reality by a refusal to act on some decision. ("Should I leave?" "Should I ask the boss for a raise?" "Should I confront my husband?") Psychologists have found that the decision you make is minimally important. What is important is what you do after you make the decision. Whether to have children or not, for example, isn't as important as what you do after you make the decision. You can have children and choose to accept, or resist, the interruption, messes, and demands on your time—that's what will create your experiences.

Similarly, you can decide not to have children and choose to accept or resist the remarks of others, the change in relationship with friends who have children, and your childfree life-style. It is your actions after you make the decision that will determine your emotional experiences.

Get second opinions

You may have friends and acquaintances that support your lack of acceptance ("That's terrible"; "You should be angry about that"; "You're right, they're wrong."). Make a habit of associating with people who are objective or who have a more acceptance-oriented, action-oriented, and tell-the-truth-oriented point of view. A lot is made of being empathic with others. In fact, an empathic response is likely to keep a person in that particular feeling experience. This may be ok in some types of relationships, but it can actually be a negative in a therapeutic relationship. Therapists are generally trying to help others move to a different level of feeling; this is hampered by empathy.

If you have been keeping your problem a secret, you can benefit by telling others about it, thus indicating that you're choosing to accept it. If, on the other hand, you have been excessively discussing your problem, you might find talking to yourself out loud more helpful.

Keep your attention on your vision

Successful people accept setbacks in stride. Disappointments rarely stop them from getting what they want. By holding onto your vision in the face of disappointments, you also will find that more people will want to help and support you, because they see you are serious. This is how you develop fans and loyalty:

Shrug off setbacks and move on. Don't let disappointment cause you to scrap your vision.

Accept setbacks as setbacks, not as failures or defeats.

Keep your focus on your vision and see the setback as a friendly guidepost ("This way" to another course, one that is usually shorter and easier).

See disappointment as a momentary point on the path to success. Project yourself into the future (Looking back, I see it was really the best thing that could have happened to me").

Assume that retrospection will reveal a current problem to be a blessing—in fact, this is usually the case. {There is a story about an old man in an Asian country who becomes much richer over night when a bunch of wild horses passed through his farm, and several of the horses decided to stay on. The villagers came to the old man and congratulated him on his fortune. The old man listened but when they were through, he questioned, "Is that good?" Several weeks down the road his son decided to break some of the horses and exchange them for real money. In the process he was thrown, and he broke his arm. Again, he was visited and everyone expressed condolences for the son's injury. When they have finished the old man asked, "Is that bad?" Not long after the incident, the community the old man lived in went to war with a neighboring community and the military come by conscripting all the able-bodied young men into service. His son could not go because of his broken arm.}

Develop the self-faith and resilience to make disappointments serve you. Get knocked down six times; get up six times.

Go with the flow. The shortest distance between two points isn't always a straight line but may be the line of least resistance.

Take the setback, not as a superstitious "sign" that you won't get what you want, but as necessary feedback.

Recover quickly from disappointments. Minimize the amount of time you're on the mat. When you wait for the full count of ten, you miss out on opportunities that current reality has to offer. You usually have "golden time" right after a disappointment, during which you can redirect your course.

Go the extra half inch. The difference between success and failure is often small, but that half inch can be so difficult that most people don't complete it. It is said that the difference between the average person and the expert is about 15%.

Be willing to do everything you must to accept your current reality, and create what you want. You don't have to do everything; just be willing to do everything. If you are willing to walk through every open door that you need to, follow every new path, take advantage of each opportunity, you can create what you want.

HOW TO CREATE WHAT YOU WANT

To create the experiences you want, you need to connect where you are (current reality) with where you want to go (your vision). Your vision guides the actions you should take in current reality. Your vision is the magnet that does the pulling—you simply allow it to materialize.

I decided when I was five years old I wanted to be a doctor who worked with the mind. It was another ten to fifteen years before I learned that the type of doctor was called a psychiatrist. That image guided me through how I approached my studies (I was co-valedictorian of my high school class), how involved I became with my girlfriends (too many of my friends were starting families before they were even out of high school), what type of school I chose, (you could get expelled from the school I went to for driving a car-but the academic reputation allowed me to get into medical school after only three years), and how I chose to relate to my parents (The only rule I can recall as an adolescent was that I was expected to get up in the morning the first time my father called me to do so—by today's standards very early—and I did what I was expected to do). Everything lined up over time, and I was eventually able to call myself a doctor and psychiatrist. There were many opportunities to deviate from the vision as you might expect.

Lights, camera, action

You can use four steps to create what you want:
    Acknowledge where you are (tell the truth).
    Create an image of what you want and visualize it happening.
    Let the "how" of going from Step One to Step Two happen naturally.
    Light up where you are, picture what you want, and act on your hunches.

Make it up

We have already covered the first step, accepting current reality. The second step is to make up what you want to create.

Many creative people believe that we have a fixed amount of creativity. F. Scott Fitzgerald believed, for example, that each writer has only a finite amount of creativity. The mistake in this thinking is confusing the finite physical world with the infinite psychological world. Creativity belongs to the psychological realm.

Highly productive, creative people such as Pablo Picasso and Steven Spielberg know that creativity is boundless. Creativity is variations on themes, and the number of themes and variations you can come up with is limitless. As long as you know you're just making it up, you can never run dry. Your ultimate choice is to make up what you want, and then create it. In the choice system, because you choose what you want, you are able to define your visions. The more clearly and specifically you define your visions, the more likely you'll achieve them.

Use the following suggestions to create visions:

Create visions, not goals. A goal is something you believe you have to do or should do that will come about in the future. Goals usually are internalizations of parents' or societal expectations. You will likely feel pushed or driven to reach goals. A vision, on the other hand, is a picture or image of something that's important to you that you want to create: You allow the vision to pull you to its realization.

Hold your vision and let go of expectations. Expectations are often a force for failure. (Elizabeth Taylor's mother pushed her expectation of becoming a star onto Elizabeth. The product was a great actress, but a woman with many apparent personal problems.) People in the change system often shift from positive expectations to negative ones in an attempt to ward off disappointment. Neither work. One of Murphy's laws is that negative expectations lead to negative results and positive expectations also lead to negative results.

Visions take little or no emotional energy (contrast visualizing winning the lottery with expecting to win the lottery). Vision is creative rather than reactive. Make the vision yours. The vision needs to be something you can create ("I feel good about my son" versus "My son has a job").

Make the assessment as detailed and clear as possible. To get a clear picture, take a deep breath, relax, close your eyes, and move your eyes up to the right corners; hold them there, and let the image you want come. You access the image source by moving your eyes in this direction. As we just mentioned, be specific-the more specific the better ("I'll grade all the exams and read two of the research papers" versus "I'll catch up on some grading"). Add some specific detail to the picture ("I see myself putting the papers in my briefcase"). Visualize what attention to your visions will feel like, look like, and sound like. Relax into the vision.

Focus on the end result, not the how. Don't focus on a specific person to create your vision—for example, a relationship with a specific customer to whom you want to sell your product. When you need specific people, the tendency is to become manipulative or desperate.

Have your cake and eat it, too. Replace either/or with and. "I can take the promotion or be relaxed and calm"; "I can be married or feel free" become "I'll take the promotion and be relaxed and calm"; "I'll be married and feel free." As long as you create your visions, why not create the best case?

Don't worry about vanity. In everything we do there is a degree of vanity. Don't let the vanity issue stop you from going for what you may want. Don't let your belief that getting what you want would be showing off, stop you, and don't let others' opinions stop you. For example, if you've lost your job but have been offered another one at a lower salary, don't let vanity stop you from reaching your vision (to be employed).

Make your vision positive instead of negative ("I'll turn the report in Friday" versus "I don't want to turn this report in late").

Don't be stupid about your visions. If you can't swim, don't make your vision to win seven gold medals in swimming at the next Olympics. While most people underestimate what they can create, a few sabotage themselves with pie-in-the-sky daydreams.

Be true to yourself

Keep the "<u>shoulds</u>" from undercutting your wants. For example, you may think you should go to graduate school, but you really want to travel. Even if what you want seems inappropriate, be true to yourself and create a vision that matters to you. It is much easier to create something you really want.

Be honest

If you don't really believe you'll do something ("Sure, I'd like to share an apartment with you"), don't say you will. Be truthful about what you want and don't want.

Develop a habit of doing only what you really want to do. You do have that freedom. Ask for what you believe you're worth. A recent study found that people who asked for a lot of money for their work usually got it, while people who asked for little got little.

The past as cause

When you're in the old, unrewarding change system, you look to the past (your parents, bad breaks, lack of education) for the cause of your present problems, and you look to the past for answers on how to create your future ("How did I do it before?"). You stir the dead ashes of the past trying to light your future.

Past solutions rarely create something new. You've never done the "new thing" before, so you don't know how to do it yet. You may at times develop plans along the way-if one plan doesn't work you let go of it and create another. The plan is always secondary to the result you want.

The future as cause

In the psychological world you're free from time constraints. You only have one time, the present, so you can play around with time in your mind. For example, you can make the future the cause of the present. You choose and envision what you want to happen in the future and let that determine what you automatically do in the present. Perhaps you envision being a doctor. As long as you hold that "future" vision, it will become the cause of what you do in the present (apply to medical school) to make it happen. After you choose the future, you're free to focus on current reality. The tension between your vision and current reality will lead you to see what needs to be done in the present to create the future.

For example, I have a vision of you reading this book. That vision becomes the cause for what IS done to bring it about. I don't know exactly how it will get from the bookstore or library to you. How isn't a major concern.

Indecision comes from needing to know how. It's the ultimate "Yes, but...." ("Yes, but how?" "How do I lose weight?" "How do I get the money?"). "How" puts the responsibility outside of you. Eliminate decision anxiety by letting the how develop spontaneously in the now.

Replace "how" ("How will I get the money and how will I get the time to go to Europe?") with "somehow" ("Right now I don't have the time or money, but somehow I'm going to Europe"). How expresses a lack of faith and increases self-doubt and undermines commitment. Somehow is a statement of faith and commitment. Making the "somehow" commitment generates the necessary "hows." To create what you want, all you ever need to do is acknowledge current reality and create a current vision. This vision will automatically move you forward. After you create your current vision, your vision becomes your current reality and you then generate a new vision. In this sense the creative process is always in flux and unstable; that is the nature of the psychological world.

Is your vision hot or cold?

The creative process works like a heat-seeking missile. Keep your vision hot and use current reality (the now) to guide you (by telling you when you're warm or cold) and you will automatically reach your vision.

Decide what you want and then keep your vision hot until you hit it; demonstrate on a continuing basis that you run the show. Practice creating what you want in life.

Your self-defeating beliefs are like brain grooves. You repeat them thousands of times until they become conditioned, habitual ways of responding to specific cues. Writer Eknath Easwaran compares our beliefs to channels in the mind. Each time you react to a belief, you dig the corresponding channel a little deeper. In the book Dialogue with Death, Easwaran says, "It is almost neurological; we are conditioning the patterns of thinking within the brain. And finally, there is a huge Grand Canal in the mind. Then anything at all is enough to provoke a conditioned response. Conscious pours down the sluice of least resistance."

Your automatic reaction is like going into a kind of trance. You overlook the actual current reality and get lost in your own version of current reality.

You can probably recognize the feeling and the corresponding thoughts ("I have to control this"; "I'll show them"; "Do they like me?"). Use these four steps when you catch yourself falling into these patterns:

1. Acknowledge your trance state. Accept and love it. Experience it for forty-five seconds and let it go ("I am in a trance state, wanting to control the situation, and I'll just acknowledge it and experience my feelings").
2. Refocus on your vision ("What do I want here?"). Choose your vision ("I choose to create it").
3. Let go of all your demands-good and bad. Keep your expectations few and your vision hot ("My vision is to feel good about myself at the party. I'm not expecting anything—that people will laugh

at my jokes, that men/women will fall all over me, that I'll control my drinking to happen or not happen").
4. Tune into the physical world. Look, touch, listen, do something. When you're in your trance, you're out of it (the physical world). Bring some real-world input into your system. Look at the world around you as if you're seeing it for the first time. Do something, anything. Get up, move around, talk to someone, smell a favorite cologne, touch a tweedy fabric or the arms of your chair.

Birds of a feather

You probably find you are attracted to or attract people who reinforce your failure habit. If you believe you have to be the star, you'll find people who "one-up" you, or who will cater to your vanity. If you are over concerned with others' approval, you'll find people who stroke you, or reject you.

Don't take success personally

Most of us are highly vulnerable to going off course after some success or movement toward our vision. People frequently take success personally ("I am a star"; "I am in control"; "I am lovable"), lose sight of their vision, and stop their forward progress.

Keep your vision pure

Serve the vision, not your beliefs ("I want a new car just to have a new car, not to prove that I'm a worthy, powerful, and successful person"). Keep your motivation at the highest possible level. Create your vision for the joy of it, the love of it, the beauty of it, or the truth of it, rather than to show others, or yourself, that you aren't a loser. When your motivation is based on a dysfunctional belief, you end up strengthening that belief, not dispelling it.

When you are moving toward creating what you want, you'll generally feel good, interested, and enthusiastic. When your mood jumps up to exhilaration, however, you need to make sure you haven't lost sight of current reality and gone into a trance. You may need to re-ground yourself in physical reality.

If you're successful, it is because of what you're doing, not because of who you are. When you go off on side issues, you not only lose your vision but you reinforce the beliefs that cause your failures and emotional distress.

The idea of control, like change, is confusing because control does happen to operate in many situations in the physical world (for example, the carburetor controls the flow of gas in your car). But in the psychological world, your opportunities for choice are in flux, constantly increasing and decreasing. Sometimes choices are available and at other times they are unavailable. If your boss refuses to give you time off, he is not controlling you; he has merely taken away one of your choices (your choice to leave with his permission—you still have the choice to leave without his permission and accept the consequences).

Look for transfers

Once you move into the choice system, options begin to appear that you never suspected you had. But remember the choice system is not magic. Rarely do you have one clear path to get what you want. You usually need to use several avenues to get where you want to go. If you're willing to take only a nonstop flight to Nome, Alaska, from Little Rock, Arkansas, you'll probably never get there. Rarely do you have perfect solutions, or one-way flights; more often you have a series of partial solutions that eventually get you what you want.

Substitute vision makers for vision killers

Instead of following habitual thinking pattern ("Someone will slam a door in my face") decide to keep your commitment. Commitment is valuing your vision enough to make it happen. Its opposite is contempt, a vision killer. Contempt is devaluing your vision to make yourself feel better. Devaluing your vision ("Who wants to own a house?" "Houses are too much trouble") throws you off course. Similarly, because you are always part of your vision, devaluing yourself ("I was too stupid to buy a house when the market was good") destroys your vision. The old Groucho Marx joke about not wanting to join a club that would accept him illustrates a subtle way to devalue yourself: "I wouldn't want someone or something (a job, mate, or house) that would have me." The moral: Stay away from contempt.

Be on the lookout for the three other vision killers:

1. Why? -"Why do I want the aggravation and responsibility of owning a house?"
2. What if? -"What if Sue or I lose our jobs and can't make the payments?"
3. How? -"How will we ever find a house we can afford?"

Paul learned to replace the three deadly vision breakers with three vision makers:

1. Why not? "Why not buy a house? It's what I want." A character in one of George Bernard Shaw's plays said, "Some people look at what is and say, 'Why?' I look at what might be and say, 'Why not?'"
2. So what? "So, what if one of us loses our job? We'll get another one." So, what is accepting and thereby freeing yourself to get what you want.
3. Somehow "Somehow we'll find a house we can afford." How is doubt; somehow is faith. Faith and patience are important because you use them while you hold on to your vision.

The benefits of telling others what you want outweigh the disadvantages. Saying what you want reaffirms your commitment and increases your resources. You find that other people are a gold mine of information.

But don't use public opinion to shame you into completing a task. Over the long run this will backfire by making others' opinions more important than your own. Take the suggestions of others only if they are compatible with what you want.

Avoid the cosmic myth

A frequent stumbling block when you start to create your own life is the belief that the universe will automatically provide you with what you need. The reasoning is that if you just picture what you want and release it to the cosmos, universal forces will automatically manifest what you want in your life. This is magical thinking, the type of thinking children often engage in. When what you wish for doesn't appear, you go to the opposite extreme and believe you can't create anything.

To create what you want, you are the one who must make it happen. You have to create a vision, choose to have it happen, and do whatever is necessary to make it happen. As you become better at this process, you will be able to make your visions happen earlier and more easily. At times, achieving your visions may seem magical, because you don't know how it happens, or why. The right opportunities begin to appear at the perfect time. The reason is that, as your awareness expands, you'll be able to see more of the choices and opportunities that were always there.

The rich get richer

As you become familiar with the psychological principles of self-creation, you will have an accelerating rate of success.

Rock bottom change versus rock bottom choice

As you move toward your vision, you will nearly always encounter some setbacks and obstacles. In the choice system, setbacks are creative forces that propel you toward your vision. Setbacks are opportunities to reaffirm your vision and to be true to yourself.

Rock bottom is where you think you have to hit before you can start to get better. Many people say they had to "hit rock bottom" before they could bounce back. In the change system, you free-fall until you hit rock bottom. You have to wait until your life is a total mess, before you decide to quit drinking. You know that you will hit, but where? And when? In the choice system you define your rock bottom. To hit rock bottom, simply accept current reality.

ACT; don't react

Robert Fritz, in his book *Path of Least Resistance*, teaches that "structural tension"—focusing on both current reality and your vision at the same time—is necessary for you to create what you want. Accept where you are and go for what you want. The vision you choose (being successful at your job, having a successful relationship) feeds back on current reality, and it makes the reality lighter, warmer, easier to accept. Taking action to create your vision helps to complete the acceptance process, and it reinforces your commitment to your vision by reaffirming its value.

Making a critical choice

With patience, you will start to make more critical choices; choices that more quickly create the experience you want. Mess things up to break your failure pattern. If you want to bake a cake that tastes good, you have to follow the right recipe. If you keep baking a cake that fails, something's wrong with the recipe; you have to modify it. You might have to add more eggs, or put in less flour. In life, people often keep using the same recipe (failure pattern) and are surprised and upset when failure keeps coming out in the same distasteful way. You need to alter the recipe (your choices) to have your life come out the way want. If you can't think of anything to alter, mess up the recipe—do something different. You're bound to get a different outcome.

The critical choice for one person's happiness may be to leave their job; for another, the critical choice may be to stay. When you use the ACT Formula, critical choices start to appear. Often you have to start moving before a critical choice becomes clear. The ACT Formula gets you moving.

Farsighted creativity

If you're temperamentally farsighted, you're probably great at fantasy and at coming up with brilliant ideas. You have trouble with the details, however, and don't see the obstacles that are in front of you. When you run into difficulties, you forget your original vision, because it's more fun to conjure up a new vision. To strengthen your new vision:

- Hold one aim at a time. Once you start a project (cleaning the garage), don't start anything else until you have finished it.
- Pay attention to current reality. Develop the habit of describing where you are now: the sights, sounds, smell, and sensations of the moment. If you are stopped in rush hour traffic in the middle of the freeway, for example, take a moment to describe the physical reality to yourself ("I smell the gasoline exhaust; I feel the smooth plastic of the steering wheel; I hear music on the radio").
- Focus on what you're doing when you're doing it. When you get gas for your car turn all your thoughts toward getting gas. Think about each step as you do it (turn the pump on, fill the tank, replace the hose and cap).
- Take the frontal position. Face what you fear. Move toward what you want to avoid. If you have important phone calls to make, make the one you dread the most first.
- Act more and think less. Spend less time thinking about what you are going to do, and do it instead.
- Talk less and do more. Talk can lull you into thinking you're taking action.
- Sell yourself on the value of taking care of details. Stop putting down people you consider to be "plodders" or "grinds." Begin to value them instead. Look at the results they create by paying attention to detail. Notice how they use detail to get them what they want (as opposed to using detail for its own sake).
- Imagine less and see more. Focus more on your surroundings and on the task at hand than on your succession of ideas. Tune in more to the physical world and less to the psychological.

Nearsighted creativity

Your problem may be the opposite; you get cemented in current reality. You see so many potential problems in getting started, that you never do begin.

Your feet are so firmly planted on the ground that you can't lift them. All you can see is what's around you. You have no vision to pull you forward. You may also have trouble finishing, because that would mean you would have to start a new project.

Practice the following methods to improve your far vision: imagine more and think less. Practice imagining the ideal way you would like your vision to turn out. If you're working on a project, hold a vision of its completion. Don't visualize the worst and try to overcome it with self-discipline; because, this method depletes energy. When you visualize the worst, you spend energy on worry, anxiety, and fear. Even the most ardent self-discipline can't produce results from fatigue and stress.

Take more risks

Jump in and see what happens. Try things out. Err on the side of inclusion. Better to make a fool of yourself than to miss an opportunity to get what you want.

Develop more faith, and assume that you will reach your vision. Don't worry about how; just begin to take action in faith. If you're working hard toward your vision, you're probably doing something wrong. You can always correct your course as you go along. If you don't like your course, you can always let go of it and try something else.

Sell yourself on visualizing. Look at great "imaginers" in our culture (Walt Disney, George Lucas, Dr. Martin Luther King, Jr., Lee Iacocca) and see what they've accomplished.

Look at people who succeeded rather than those who failed. Find success stories to read. Go to success movies about people who don't let current reality block their visions (Gandhi).

Take time to daydream. As you start, ask yourself, "What do I want?" or "What would I like to see happen?"

Make starts at imperfect times. Rather than starting to create a thin body on Monday morning, begin it in the middle of a gourmet meal. Start your book before you have the word processor. Teach yourself that everything in your environment doesn't have to be perfect for you to begin.

How to achieve 20/20 Vision

You need both far and near vision to create what you want. You need to be a visionary, and you need to focus on details. Keep your broad perspective and improve your focusing ability. If you find yourself giving too much attention to either your near, or your far vision, attempt to balance your vision.

Willpower

In the change system you create negative feelings ("They are making me go to the meeting, and I don't want to go"), and then you use your will to overcome these bad feelings ("I'll force myself to go"). Lack of willpower is a common excuse for blaming in the change system ("I'm just lazy"; "He lacks willpower").

In the change system you continually have to inject yourself with willpower to overcome your internal resistances. Willpower may work for you, but you pay a high price. You lose your spontaneity and sense of fun, and you develop third-degree burnout.

A common mistake is to run an event through the "worst case" machine ("I'll get cancer"). You do this to generate some anxiety so that you will be motivated to react and avoid the worse case ("I have to stop smoking"). This strategy seldom works, because you can't keep up the steady flow of negative images.

Imagination is more powerful than willpower. The image ("Wouldn't a cigarette taste good?") wins out over the willpower to stop smoking. To stop the conflict within yourself, imagine what you want to have ("I imagine healthy lungs and deep breaths"), and then decide that you'll create it.

Consider the big and small choices. The big choice is to have a clear desk; the small choice is to take some action to clean it (throw out old message slips, put paper clips away). Once you make the big choices, priorities are set. Once you make the big choice, the smaller ones that support it become easier to make. Your big choice will guide you. The trick is to keep your eye on current reality and on where you want to go.

Manage Your Focus

Negative feelings become ingrained when you give in to them and you stop knowing what you want. You can develop your ability to shift your attention to what you want.

Get to know your focus. Watch for times when you are able to direct your focus ("I'm tired and I'm choosing to get my homework done").

Use positive language. Start describing your visions in "choice" terms. ("I choose to finish it" versus "I'll try." "I choose to" versus "I can." "I choose not to do it" versus "I can't.")

Accept discomfort

Whenever you find yourself in an uncomfortable situation (anxiety, fatigue, physical pain), choose to accept it, and put your focus on the experience you want. If you feel anxious about going to a party, accept your anxiety, then focus on the experience you want to have ("I'm anxious, but I am going to think about having a good time"). If you want to get your midterm paper done, but have a roaring headache, turn your focus to the experience you want ("I accept that I have a headache, but I'm going to focus on getting the paper done").

Start a program

Start a systematic program such as aerobics or meditation. Structured programs can help develop your ability to direct your focus to your big choice.

Stretch

Stretch your image of what you can accomplish ("I will give the talk"; "I will take a trip on my own"). In golf, if you always putt short, you never make your shot. If you putt long, you sometimes make it.

Do what you fear

If you want to avoid some activity, or person, because of fear, step over the fear instead of bowing down to it. Focus your attention on what you want, even though you fear the process of getting there. "I'm afraid to drive but I am going to focus on going to the grocery store to get what I want without having to rely on my neighbor." "I'm afraid to ask for a raise but I'm going to focus on the raise I want." "I'm afraid of being alone tonight, but I am going to focus on creating a good evening, when I can to enjoy a good book and a cup of hot chocolate."

Drop tasks to train your focus

When you're doing something, and your husband, wife, or child asks you to do something else, stop, and do it. Instead of saying, "Just a minute, I want to finish this," drop your task and do his or hers. When you have to hold your focus on a dropped task until you get back to it, you practice directing your focus to what you want.

Practice focused listening

Whenever anyone talks to you—your family, your clients, sales people—focus attentively on what they are saying. Attentive listening will help you improve your focus, and it is a success force in its own right. People are attracted to people who genuinely listen to them.

Keep your vows

Make fewer promises to yourself and others, and keep those you do make. If you decide to finish a project, finish it even though you've lost your motivation for it. Breaking your word, even to yourself, erodes your ability to hold your vision.

Use self-exams

If you listen to your secretary with only one ear, be honest to yourself about your inattentiveness. If you really read magazines in your office all day, don't tell people how hard you worked on preparing next year's budget.

People who are extraordinary in any field usually have the ability to slow down their mind enough to focus on what is in front of them. They can concentrate. The star tennis player sees the ball at about half the speed others do. When you use your focus to create what you want, you slow your mind down in the same way.

Practice Directing Your Focus

With practice you're able to create your vision more quickly. When you make choices and act on them, you become smarter, you develop "tacit" knowledge that you can bring to new situations.

Robert Sternberg, a psychologist at Yale, has been looking at intelligence in new ways. To him, intelligence is getting what you want, and getting what you want depends on "tacit" knowledge, knowledge that has never explicitly been taught. Most of the knowledge that you need to succeed on your job you pick up on your own. Promotions and raises often depend on how well you've picked up specific knowledge. People are successful in making friends or producing hit records, because they have this knowledge to draw upon. With practice, you can develop tacit knowledge in any area.

Imagine that you stop by the bakery to get a chocolate chip cookie every night. One day you decide to make a big choice to weigh less and a small choice to stop eating your nightly cookie. The first time you walk by the bakery, accept the reality that you're hungry, and you are choosing to go by without getting a cookie. You may be uncomfortable, but the next time will be a little less difficult, because you gained tacit knowledge from the first act. After you have practiced directing your focus for a year, and you have walked by the bakery 250 times, you will probably find it more difficult to buy a cookie than to pass it by. Practice makes creating new experiences easier, even if you have relapses in between.

Relationships often develop through tacit knowledge. You learn what it is that people like and dislike by being with them and paying attention to them. You can't learn from a book that a certain man or woman disapproves of off-color jokes, but if you spend time with that person, you learn about that particular characteristic. If you accept that you are afraid to develop relationships and then take actions to be with people anyway, you will learn the tacit knowledge that will help you develop relationships. Like learning to walk by a bakery without buying the cookie, it becomes easier and easier with practice. The more you practice being with people, the easier it becomes to relate to all people.

Enjoy yourself

Remember, the idea was to enjoy yourself. You chose your job, mate, and the place where you live to create more enjoyment for yourself. Creating what you want should not be a chore. If you're working hard and deriving no pleasure from it, you're doing something wrong. Instead of seeing your vision at the top of a mountain you must struggle to climb, see your vision downstream, and enjoy the float down to it. Periodically, remind yourself to enjoy the process. Creating your own life is an ongoing process, not a series of life events.

Be true to your vision

Use the strategies you need to keep your vision hot and your sight clear. Some will work better than others for you, but practice always works. Your path from current reality to your vision is paved with action.

Take action

You can wait or you can act. You can wait to study for the bar when your virus is gone, or you can study despite your virus. You can wait to have a home until you find a husband, or wife, or you can create a home as a one-person family. You can wait to go to the movie until someone asks you, or you can ask someone to go.

Don't wait

Create your happiness now. Waiting shoves action to the future—when your headache is gone, or you're married, or you're made happy by someone else. Waiting robs the present of the creative possibilities. To create the moments that you want, you have to act in the moment, not in the future. Alice Koller, a Ph.D. in philosophy from Harvard, spent the first thirty-seven years of her life waiting. She became sick of her life-style and decided to spend a winter alone in Nantucket, searching for the source of her unhappiness. In her journal, *The Unknown Woman*, she meticulously recorded her discoveries. "Waiting? Why? The stupendous thing I used to wait for was something that was going to be done to me, or for me: to be initiated by someone else, independent of my choice. But there isn't someone else to make things happen to me. I'm the only person who can do what I decide needs to be done. And besides, there is no reason for anyone else to do anything at all for me, particularly something as glorious as that thing I expected. Waiting is irrelevant on two counts. There is nothing to wait for, because I'll initiate what happens to me. There is nothing to wait for, because these minutes now passing are my life. They are the minutes in which my living is to be done. Whatever I do, I'll do in my own time and I will do it. I don't have to wait to get married to have a home: I'll make my own. I don't have to wait for someone to give me a sense of continuity; I'll carry my continuity within myself. I'll belong wherever I am. I'll institute my own permanence." Waiting is part of the unrewarding change system. When you want something to change (your feelings, your job, the weather, the lonely weekend, your parents, your spouse, your life), you wait. You wait for the curtain to open and your life to begin. You believe something or someone will come along and make you happy. And so, you wait."

When you wait (put off action), you spend your "waiting time" thinking about the future. You either worry, or you hope. Although worry seems bad and hope seems good, neither will get you what you want if you don't take action in the present. Surprisingly, worry and hope feed on one another. You worry that what you hope for won't happen, and you hope that what you worry about won't happen.

Worry-mobile

In the change system, you drive a worry-mobile. You have a worry of the day, worry of the week, worry of the year, and worry of a lifetime. You operate on worry fuel. When you run low, you fill your tank with more ("There must be some ominous reason why things are going so well"). Sometimes you have so much worry you need a trailer to haul it around. You may ask others to take a spin in your worry-mobile ("Don't you think it's a bit odd everything seems to be going so smoothly?"). You create worry through internal combustion. You imagine the worst ("I could go bankrupt") and then react to this image ("That would be terrible"; "I couldn't stand that"). The resulting clash between your images and your reactions creates worry and anxiety. Once you crank up enough worry, you become motivated to do something about the problem ("I'd better go out and make a sale") to get rid of the worry. Once you stop worrying (imagining the worst), you lose your motivation. You may achieve some success with worry, because it is a powerful motivator. But, the cost per mile is high.

Hope-mobile

If you wait instead of act, you have another car in the garage alongside your worry-mobile. This car seems more desirable because it's a hope-mobile, but it too can keep you from acting in the present. The hope-mobile is fueled by "it"-the perfect mate, the big break, the right job, the smaller dress size, the ultimate date. Hope is waiting for "it." Your life is based on the illusion that when you get "it" you will be happy. Workaholics, for example, have the illusion that when they finish their project they will be free. The idea of freedom is the "it" that fuels their hope-mobile. Rather than making a choice to work or a choice to be free, they overwork to get freedom, which is always just out of their reach. Philosophers have said for over two thousand years, "Happiness cannot be measured by what we have, but only by freedom from wants."

How Goals Rip You Off

Waiting for "it" is how you get ripped off by goals. "When I'm out of school [or in school] I'll be happy." You give the goal the power to dictate your feelings. If you don't reach the goal, if it's less than what you thought, or if you realize that you're still the same person you were before you reached it, the goal you set makes you unhappy. It rips you off. It promises but doesn't deliver. You may think you won't be happy until you find your identity, so you spend years looking for it. You conclude you won't feel fulfilled until you know your true calling, so you live each minute looking for it. In the choice system, you have visions, but you don't make the visions responsible for your feelings. You don't hope for something that might, or might not, occur to make you happy. You simply decide what you want (to be in graduate school) and take action to achieve it (work nights to earn tuition, study German to get a jump on the Ph.D. requirements, apply to schools you can afford, visit each school to find out about financial aid and work-study grants). You are already doing what you need to do to get what you want. You are a master practicing, not someone practicing to be a master.

Goal directed behavior vs. process directed behavior

Individuals who are focused on goals will have very intense short periods of joy that are spaced between huge intervals of time. Those who are process oriented are more likely to enjoy the trip. They smell the roses along the way. They enjoy the goal, but it is only one part of the trip, and not everything.

After you make it up, create it

In the choice system, rather than looking for "it," you "make it up" (what you want) and then create it ("Instead of looking for a job, I'll create one"), If you don't like your first creation, you make up something else. For example, you may have created a vision of establishing a successful relationship with a particular person, but then you find the other person isn't interested in you. So you discard this specific vision and develop a vision of having a relationship where you receive love as well as give love. However a vision is not something you discard lightly. If you keep discarding your vision, usually when you meet obstacles, you will never get what you want. You design your own life. Rather than looking for the right path for you, decide what you want, and build your own path to it.

Waiting is passive

When you wait for other people to act, you put your life on hold. You give the other person (or situation) power over you. If you must wait, make a conscious choice to wait. By making a conscious choice to wait, we move the event from a passive experience to an active one.

Waiting Is Painful

The Supreme Court ruled that it is humane to execute a criminal, but it is cruel and unusual punishment to make that person wait to be executed. Because waiting is aversive, you try to avoid as much waiting as possible; you eventually become aggressive to get rid of the resentment. You may use waiting as a weapon. You make others wait the way you had to wait. When you are the pilot, it is customary to ask for a further clearance time, if you are asked to wait at a specific point during the flight. If a FCT (further clearance time) is not asked the person could fly over that point until they run out of gas and fall out of the air. This is exactly what people do in their life. They wait until they self-implode. People will wait until anger, or revenge, takes over. Next time you plan to meet a friend for lunch, ask them for an FCT—a time that you can go ahead and order or make other arrangements.

> Sometimes waiting is a manipulation.
> Waiting is always wasteful.

Watch your waiting

You will find it helpful to become aware of your waiting moments. I bet you will be surprised at how much time you spend waiting each day. If you drive on the highways in any of the large cities don't forget to add in those moments of no forward motion while in your car. Then there are the lines at the DMV, or at the grocery store. Keep counting.

White balls & black balls

Waiting can be focusing on what you can't do ("Make a publishing agent like my work") and overlooking what you can do ("Choose to acknowledge myself because I write every day"). Success comes when your desired choices are your actual choices. You may have many actual choices of which you are unaware. Attending writers' workshops and conferences could result in meeting writers and publishers who might then introduce you to an agent.

You also have many pseudo-choices, or illusions. When you are aware of real choices, you can create success, because that is where you have response ability. To clarify, call your unaware actual choices white balls. Call your illusionary choices black balls. When you're trying to change something, if you focus on black balls (past and future) and ignore the white ones (the present) you do not get anywhere. You may believe you should be able to do what you can't ("I need to turn the clock back"), or you believe you can't do what you can ("I can't accept that"). When you are operating from choice, you select the white 'can do' balls (make a phone call, talk to your boss, and learn about the housing situation). You merge believed choices—what you believe you can do—with actual choices. In other words, you see and accept more current reality.

Divide and act

As you raise your awareness of waiting, it's helpful to separate white balls from black ones. If you want a specific person to marry you, and the person doesn't want to, label that a black ball and throw it away. Ask yourself what your white balls are—join a singles group, join a travel club, get on a coed softball team, or join a choir. You can't choose to have someone propose to you. You can dress nicely, talk to people of the opposite sex, and ask someone out. Whether that person agrees is his or her choice (your black ball), but you can choose to ask (white ball).

You can eliminate waiting

Suppose you are in a long supermarket line. If you're in the unrewarding change system, you wait and make yourself uncomfortable ("Won't this line ever speed up?" "Oh no, that lady has a lot of coupons"; "Stupid checker can't even push the right keys!"). Waiting is a self-generated, uncomfortable psychological experience. You can replace your uncomfortable psychological experience of waiting by taking action in the present. You do this by using the ACT Formula:

You accept current reality ("I am uncomfortable and in a long, slow line"). You choose and envision the experience you want ("I'll enjoy myself, and I will get checked out as quickly as possible"). You take action to create your vision. Your actions will depend on the current reality.

> To take action in the present, you might:
> Look for a shorter line.
> Leave the store and come back when it's not so busy.
> If you have a few items, ask if you could move ahead of the person with two big baskets.
> Ask the manager to open another cash register.
> Tune into your surroundings and observe people.
> Strike up a conversation with someone in the line.
> Balance your checkbook.
> Read the magazines and newspapers at the checkout counter until your turn comes.

The actions you take will often be largely unconscious. After you accept where you are and choose your vision, you do what seems right. You may have the ability to rearrange the physical world (move to an express aisle), but at times you will be in a situation in which all the lines are six deep.

Being in the choice system doesn't necessarily mean you get checked out any faster. You can, however, always create a different psychological experience for yourself. I use headphones to listen to an audio book, or will write out a list of the things I need to do next, in the time I have. I have over the years started carrying a bag (actually a purse) with me that contains things like a cassette player, audiotapes, a camera, and a pad, so I can jot down thoughts for endeavors like this book. I have done this so long, I don't know how I could get along without it. Women know the benefits of a purse. Men gave them up some time after the frontier days. Bad choice. Bad choice.

Be thankful

When I find myself caught up in an experience, I could be unhappy with (Being behind an accident, or in a long line) I try to identify things to be thankful about (That I have a nice car, a place to go, and that I am safe—that the line is long because there are so many good things available for each of us to buy).

Strategies for taking action

When all is said and done, much is said, and little is done. To reap the rewards of the rapid relief principles, you have to put them into action.

Be in the moment. Pay attention to what you are doing, as you do it. Don't wait for what you believe is making you unhappy to go away, or for what you believe will make you happy to come. Attend to and savor the job in front of you. Once you stop over-identifying with the physical world ("I lost my job, so I have to feel bad"), you can start to connect with the energy in the physical world ("I lost my job, but I will take action to feel good by paying attention to each task at hand in the present"). When you rake your lawn or wash your car, you can experience energy coming to you—if you choose to be open, tune in, and focus on the job. By seeing and touching the physical world, you eliminate your painful psychological self-absorption. Focus on current reality for a few minutes whenever you feel bad. If you are doing the dishes, savor the feel of the suds on a plate, the warmth of the water on your hands, the steam against your face. If you are writing out bills, listen to the sound of your checks as you rip them out. Taste the glue of the envelope and the stamps. Your five senses tell you about the now—your current reality. Tune in to them and savor what they tell you.

Jump in and take a risk

Behind your fear of taking a risk is usually the fear of being blamed by yourself, and others. When you take a risk, you step out from the crowd, and you are an easy target for blame. A new Yellow Cab driver asked one of the seasoned drivers if he had any advice for him. The old-timer said, "I have only one piece of advice. If you see an accident, no matter what, don't stop." The new driver asked why. The old-timer said, "The only thing the witnesses will remember seeing is a Yellow Cab." People who take risks are like Yellow Cabs. You cannot escape blame. If you don't start the business, people will blame you ("You never follow through"); if you start the business, they will blame you; if it is a failure, they say, "You should have known better"; and if it's successful, they say, "You're just money hungry." When you're in the choice system, the fear of blame doesn't stop you. Use the ACT Formula, if necessary, to get started:

Accept your current reality ("I accept the fact that I'm afraid people will blame me if I make the wrong decisions").

> Choose what you want and visualize it ("I see this working out great"). Take action ("I'll do it this way").

Create and correct.

You may be waiting until everything is perfect before you start moving toward your vision. You could wait forever. Start creating what you want, and correct your course as you go along.

Act and adjust

Earlier we talked about making up a vision that truly matters to you. When you have a vision that works for you (for example, developing a successful relationship), you will reach it more quickly if you are willing to make adjustments along the way (joining a health club didn't work because everyone was too busy to talk, so you join a literary club instead). You rarely create anything without the need for some adjustments along the way. Don't worry beforehand about how you will make the corrections—that's a detail. What you'll need to know will occur spontaneously, according to the demands of current reality. Maxwell Maltz, in his classic book *Psycho-Cybernetics*, says you have to trust the creative process. Don't jam it by worrying whether or not it will work, or by trying to force it. He says, "You must 'let it' work rather than 'make it' work. This trust is necessary because your creative mechanism operates below the level of consciousness, and you cannot 'know' what is going on beneath the surface." "Create and correct" is a letting go process. You have to let go of what isn't true to your vision. In a study of young artists, researchers found that the artists who were open to correcting their work were still artists twenty-five years later. Those who would not or could not, adjust their work after feedback eventually left the field of art altogether.

A successful screenwriter in Hollywood has one word on the license plate of his expensive Mercedes—REWROTE. Write your script and be willing to rewrite when current reality demands it.

Forget the perfect moment

Start taking action and adjust along the way. I believe I read once that the first flight to the moon was off tract about 80 percent of the time—but they made it.

Stop on a dime

In his book *Constructive Living*, innovative psychotherapist David Reynolds says, "Run to the edge of the cliff and stop on a dime." This sentence contains all the advice you need to eliminate waiting for some uncontrollable event. You "run (you become active and do what needs to be done) to the edge of the cliff" (you extend yourself to your potential) "and you stop on a dime" (after you have done all that you are going to do, you release the situation, and let it go). Then move on to your next project.

Use timers to help you "stop on a dime." For example, if you are waiting for dinner to cook, set a timer. Then focus on what you are doing until you hear the timer go off. If you are waiting to hear about a project, set up a mental timer, or mark it on your calendar ("If I don't hear from them in two weeks, I'll call them"), and then let it go.

Do it now

You may be waiting because you believe you have a thousand years in which to accomplish your dreams. Buddha said, "Where are those who forget death will come to all; for those who remember, quarrels come to an end." If you keep in mind how short life is, you'll stop quarreling with current reality and waiting for it to change, and you will start creating the life you want. Decide what is important and start doing it. Don't wait until you have enough time, money, or confidence to do it.

Tell the truth quickly. State what you want. Ask questions if you need to clear up confusion. Being honest is the antidote for passive-aggressive waiting, whether you are the victim or the victimizer:

"You told me you would call me last week and you didn't. What's the story?"

"I didn't finish the annual report on time, because I was angry about being passed over for the promotion."

"You told me you wanted to see me again, and then you didn't invite me to your party. What's the reason?"

"I came on strong at the meeting, because I felt intimidated by the office manager, and I didn't want it to show."

Focus on can do's

You usually have choices, even if you don't have the precise choice you want. Focus on what you can do, and you will find that other choices will start to appear.

Forget square one

Square One is another name for the change system. Relapses (stepping back into the change system) grow out of the illusion that you, or others, change. "I've fallen back to Square One" is a common expression of discouragement when your expectations are unmet. But "Square One" implies that you must struggle up through Square Two, Square Three, Square Four, and so on until you're back to where you started—and then you can start for your vision. But there is no Square One, and there aren't any other squares through which you have to struggle either. When you think you have fallen back into Square One, you have simply slipped back into needing to change the world. Either you think the world needs to change for you to be happy, or you know that you create your own life by choices. You don't have to struggle from Square One to Square Two and on up through square after square to get where you want. You simply switch your focus from change to choice. When you do you are already moving toward your vision. Once you become aware of going in and out of the change system, you can use your relapse experiences as a way to become wiser and a way to avoid the change trap next time.

Dr. Kubler Ross discusses the different phases (steps) of grief. I experience that people can, and do, go from event directly to the last step (acceptance). Going through all the other steps is merely one path you can take. I personally see the path she advocates like a circle. There is the event, then the various steps and then there is acceptance. But look again. Do you notice that acceptance is right next to the event? You just have to go in the correct direction to get there immediately.

So what—keep going

"So what" is effective because it keeps your feelings from having power over you. "Keep going" is a self-direction to act. Remember; your feelings change from moment to moment and have little to do with what you want. "So, what—keep going" keeps you moving to your vision. You might get bogged down in the middle of the journey. You may feel that you're farther from the vision than when you started. If you tell yourself, "So what," and keep going, you will find you move closer to creating your vision—and you will start feeling good again. If you get so discouraged that you stop altogether, you'll never get there. But if you tell yourself, "I get bogged down for a while. So what—keep going," you will eventually create your objective.

A variation of "So what—keep going" is "So what—do it anyway." No matter what your current reality (a headache, depression, a tyrannical boss, memories of an abusive childhood), do what you have to do. For example, "I'm afraid I'll be rejected if I apply for this job": So what—do it anyway. "I hate to write out bills": So what—do it anyway. "I can't study when I have a cold": So what—do it anyway. When the boss is tyrannical, I get so depressed I can't make myself work": So what—do it anyway. "So what" gives you choices to create the experiences you want despite your current reality. "Keep going" (or "do it anyway") moves you toward your vision. "So what—keep going" captures the essence of the choice system. It keeps you from putting your life on hold while you wait, worry, and hope.

Let go of anxiety and create self-faith

A million years ago, when humans stepped from their caves, anxiety was a good friend. Armed with nothing more than a brain, these fangless, clawless, relatively weak creatures survived because their alarm systems told them when to get out of the way, when to pick up a rock and fight, or when to freeze and not move a muscle. They triumphed over wild beasts, unpredictable weather, and antisocial enemies within their own species, because anxiety warned them of danger and signaled what to do.

Our oversensitive alarm system

We are descended from the survivors—those with the anxious genes, and the sensitive alarm systems. That's the price we pay for survival. We often live in "red alert." However, most of our survival mechanisms are actually vestiges of the past—no longer useful and often more hindrance than help. Our anxiety system is too sensitive, much like an auto burglar alarm that goes off even when no one is close to the car. We constantly over mobilize ourselves for action when there is no real danger.

Anxiety is your emotional reaction to your distorted and unrealistic appraisal of a situation. You overestimate the danger of a situation and underestimate your ability to handle it. Anxiety is acting as if ("What if?") something bad is going to happen to you.

You act as if something outside of you is responsible for your feelings, and you're helpless to do anything about it. You treat "what if" ideas ("What if I fail the test?") as if they were real and concrete. You think, feel, and act as if the feared event were occurring in the present. When you panic, you don't have awareness that the event is fictional. You believe the walls are actually closing in on you in a crowded room, or that you will jump if you get near a window. You react 'as if' your imagined dangers are real. If you know you're acting 'as if', you worry. If you forget you're acting 'as if,' you panic.

When you know that you create your own experiences, nothing outside of you "makes" you anxious. You accept responsibility for how you feel and don't blame your anxiety on anything or anyone.

Here are examples of how needing change can lead to fear:

> "My boss is to blame for my feelings, and I'm afraid I won't be able to make him like me (change him)."

> "I'm responsible for others having a good time at my party, and I'm afraid I won't be able to get them to (change them)."

> "All the people in this store are staring at me and making me nervous, and I'm afraid I won't be able to stand it (keep myself from fainting in public)."

"If I get fired, I won't be able to change how humiliated I will feel, and then I might kill myself."

"My failure to get a job is to blame for my bad feelings, and I'm afraid I'll never change this (get a job)."

Dealing with loss of choice

You are a total, interrelated organism; everything feeds back on itself. The cause creates the symptoms, and the symptoms feed back and further energize the cause. You create your anxiety by fearing your choices will be limited, and your anxiety then actually limits your choices by narrowing your awareness. By acting as if what you fear is true, you often bring it about. A good example is the often-told story of the salesman and his missing jack.

A salesman had a flat tire on a deserted highway and discovered that his jack was missing. He saw a lighted farmhouse in the distance and, thinking the farmer might have a jack, he set out for the farmhouse. As he was walking, he began to imagine that the farmer was hostile and would refuse to lend him the jack ("What if he slams the door in my face?"). The more he thought about the farmer, the more anxious he became. He then started getting angry with the farmer. By the time he got to the farmhouse, he was enraged. When the farmer answered the door, the salesman punched him in the mouth without saying a word.

Overcome anxiety with choice

The elegant way to overcome anxiety is to switch into creating your life by choice. Instead of focusing on unavailable choices or a fear of limited choices, you focus on what you want. You take responsibility for your feelings and accept the concept that, even if some future choices might be limited, you have all the choices you need to be happy and get what you want.

However, there will be times when the choice to switch out of your anxiety may be unavailable. Your primary fears ("I'll make a fool of myself") may be deeply rooted and difficult to move. Your feelings are a product of psychological and physiological brain functioning. You often can't do anything directly to alter the physical reaction or the emotions. Your mind is telling your body there is danger, and your body is reacting with the old survival mechanism of anxiety. Anxiety involves physical reactions (sweaty palms, racing heart, fainting, running away) that you may not be able immediately to alter simply by choosing not to be anxious.

AWAKE and break the trance

AWAKE consists of five steps, each one crucial to managing your anxiety. These five steps can release you from the grip of your anxiety trance:

>   Accept your anxiety.
>   Watch your anxiety.
>   Act as if you are not anxious.
>   Keep repeating these three steps until the anxiety starts to diminish.
>   Expect the unexpected, and visualize what you want.

Accept your anxiety

You can let your brain know it can turn off the red lights and silence the sirens by telling it, "Okay, I've got the message." That's acceptance. Emotions, such as your fear, are merely self-signals; messages from yourself to yourself. If you don't accept the message, the signal is intensified. If you accept the message, the signal, having served its purpose, goes away.

Needing to control what you can't control (your physical reactions) makes you feel more out of control. You escape this trap by letting go of your need to control the physical reactions. If you do this, they will soon return to their normal state. Remember, your feelings are constantly changing on their own—your attempts to change, or control, negative feelings prolong them.

Don't be alarmed by your anxiety. If you have not been bothered by strong anxiety before, or if you have not had any anxiety for a while, the anxiety may seem more dangerous to you. This is due to the sharp contrast between the anxiety state and an anxiety-free state. Just decide to accept the feelings, no matter how strange or scary they may feel.

Acceptance helps break a common anxiety spiral. Shame over showing anxiety will create more anxiety to be ashamed of showing. To break this shame-anxiety trap expose your anxiety ("I'm nervous right now") instead of trying to hide it.

Watch your anxiety

Awareness of your anxiety destroys it. Anxiety exists to make you aware, so that you heed the danger and take notice of the situation. Become aware and the anxiety has fulfilled its purpose; there is no longer a reason for its existence.

When you are in the middle of an anxiety trance, your awareness is constricted. You don't see current reality in its proper perspective. Something small ("My boss didn't speak to me") distorts to something big ("The boss hates me. He'll fire me, and I'll end up on skid row"). An aerial view would give a true picture of the situation ("My boss didn't speak to anyone in the office today").

Self-awareness is the major characteristic of your psychological world. Being able to step back and look at yourself objectively, and also look at your situation objectively, is one way you can separate the physical world (events and other people) from your psychological experiences.

When you watch your anxiety ("I am watching my anxiety about my boss's reaction to me this morning. My palms are sweaty; my mind is making up things that might happen to me; my cheeks feel flushed") you avoid getting caught up in the subjective drama of it. You bring yourself back to the present, away from an invented threatening future ("The boss is going to fire me"). When you are in the present, you are able to see available choices. (My mind is racing at this moment, but I can choose to focus on my job and do what needs to be done"; "I am aware of my anxiety and how my heart and head feel; I can choose to ask my coworker to cover the phones for me while I take a ten-minute break to relax").

Awareness of your thoughts, feelings, and actions allows you to detach, or distance, yourself from them. You create a greater sense of mastery over current reality. You can use numerous methods to improve your ability to watch your anxiety.

Watch yourself watching yourself

In extreme anxiety you do this involuntarily; it is called dissociation. Paradoxically, when you choose to do this purposefully, you can lower your anxiety. For example, imagine you are sitting on the file cabinet looking at yourself as you sit at your desk ("I am watching myself, as I become aware of my pulse, my racing heart, my feelings of dizziness"). Be outside of yourself and watch how you are performing even though you are anxious. Make your observations positive and objective ("She's putting the papers away, and she is taking care of business in an orderly way").

Put your self-instructions in positive terms. Replace beware with be aware. When you are anxious, tell yourself, "Be alert" or "Be awake" rather than "Don't be anxious." Focus on what you can do, and you will be able to decrease your sense of helplessness. Practice self-awareness when you're feeling good. Practice prepares you for times when anxiety does occur. Tune in to your current reality as often as you can. ("Right now I'm sitting in my office chair, listening to Springsteen music, and feeling warm and comfortable"). Graph the duration of your anxiety. This information can counter your tendency to think that when you are in the midst of an anxiety trance the anxiety will go on forever.

When you have objective information about your anxiety and its limits, you are better able to deal with it. When you observe your anxiety, you realize that your "peak period" lasts only so long. You may not be able to stand an anxiety that lasts forever, but you certainly can take an anxiety that is time-limited. When you know your anxiety period has a time limit, you relax. Your anxiety is automatically lessened.

Act as if you are not anxious

Your current reality responds to what you do, not to what you say, feel, or think. When you are willing to do what is necessary, you can usually create what you want. In this third step, focus on current reality and ask yourself what needs to be done to create your vision. Feel what you feel and do what needs to be done. "I accept the fact that I feel anxious. My vision is to go to the party, so I am going to get dressed to go." "I accept the fact that I feel panicked. My vision is to go to the party, so I am going to call my friend to pick me up and drive me there." "I accept the fact that I feel as if I am going to faint. My vision is to go to the party, so I am going to get into my friend's car." "I accept the fact that I feel as if I am going to faint. My vision is to go to the party, so I am going to thank my friend for the ride, get out of the car, walk up the walk, and ring the doorbell."

When you are in the middle of an anxiety trance, you often feel out of control. Your emotions and racing thoughts seem to have minds of their own. You do, however, have a say in how you move your body. No matter how anxious you are, you can still direct the long muscles in your arms and legs.

Action is the method you use to develop self-confidence and self-faith. Faith is the tool you use to deal effectively with the unknown on your way to your desired vision. Because you focus on what needs to be done (get gas, make the list of phone calls, write the memo) you indirectly switch your attention from your anxiety, and you indirectly affect your feelings. When you do the job that is in front of you, your attention shifts from "what if" to "what is." Paying attention to what is (the job at hand) helps you eliminate anxiety.

To accept your feelings as being true, and to act as if they are not, is one of the secrets of creating what you want, Accept the fact that you are anxious; act as if you are not, doing what is necessary to do in the situation. Not surprisingly, the action helps to relieve your anxiety.

If you run, your anxiety will go down temporarily, but your primary fear will go up. If you stay and face the lion, both your anxiety and your fear will go down.

You do not have to perform perfectly; just perform—in spite of the anxiety. Slow down, if you have to, but keep going. If you are talking, finish your sentences; if you are reading, continue reading; if you are driving, drive; if you are working, work. Even though you may act imperfectly, self consciously, and awkwardly, keep acting.

Keep repenting the first three steps

Each time you become anxious you have another chance to break the trance and practice the procedures:

Accept your anxiety
Watch your anxiety.
Act as if you were anxiety-free.

In other words, you keep repeating the first three steps until your anxiety goes down. This particular step in the AWAKE Strategy reminds you to develop tolerance for your anxiety. Increasing your tolerance decreases your anxiety about anxiety. By practicing, you inoculate yourself against future anxiety. People with allergies can be inoculated over and over with toxic pollens. In this way, they build tolerance in their bodies for the pollens.

Each time you experience anxiety and confront it with the first three steps of the AWAKE Strategy, you inoculate your self. When you see, through practice, that you can tolerate high levels of anxiety, you experience a sense of confidence—an antidote for anxiety,

Increase your tolerance by increasing the time lapse between feeling anxious and yielding to your habitual escape mechanisms (oversleeping, overeating, smoking, taking tranquilizers, or excessive drinking). Each anxiety experience you have serves to desensitize yourself to it. Keep in mind, as you practice the first three steps of the AWAKE Strategy, that anxiety is always time-limited and will pass more quickly if you flow with it, instead of fight it.

Expect the unexpected and focus on what you want

The worst seldom happens. This is not to say that the worst cannot happen, just that it usually doesn't. Your husband is not killed in a car accident; your son does not have leukemia; you do not have a brain tumor; you are not fired; you do not end up a homeless person. Often what happens is something you didn't count on—in terms of the everyday irrational fears that so often plague us, reality is usually friendlier than we give it credit for. People survive. If this were not true, we would not have a world population of over 4 billion people. In nearly every case, the worst does not happen.

You may believe that your worrying is what prevents the feared event from happening. On the contrary, worrying is unnecessary and unproductive thinking; it is frequently superstition. Many people even become worried because they "aren't worried." But, whatever is going to happen is going to happen whether you are worrying about it or not.

You can test this out for yourself. The next time you are worried about something, write a description of your worry in your notebook, then refuse to worry about it. When the worry returns strongly, tell yourself, "This is an experiment in living worry-free. I refuse to worry about it." Later check out your predictions. You'll find that nearly all of them don't come true. Had you allowed yourself to worry, you would have worried about nothing. Eventually you will come to realize that you don't need to worry in order to ward off bad events.

Focus on what you want to happen

Suppose you are anxious about an upcoming exam. You can worry continuously before you take the test, then worry during the test and until you get the results back. "I know I failed," you tell yourself. "I couldn't even understand some of the questions. Everyone else finished sooner than I did" If you end up passing the test, you've made yourself miserable for nothing. If you do fail the test, you would have failed it regardless of whether you had worried or not. Worrying did nothing to help you pass the test. If you visualize what you want (passing the test), your positive attitude can, at the very least, somewhat improve your performance. Because you are more relaxed when you visualize what you want, you can then focus on what needs to be done in the present. And if you fail, you fail not because you didn't worry, but because you didn't study, or because the exam was too advanced for your knowledge. Further, it is nearly impossible to tell if an apparent setback is really a setback, Time is an important ingredient in seeing the whole picture. You cannot see the future. But you can more fully enjoy the present it you accept current reality and focus on what you want to see happen. I tell my patients there is plenty of time to worry after the fact.

Create self-faith

To avoid anxiety completely you would never do anything for the first time. But life, by its nature, consists of one first-time event after another. You're constantly faced with risks, newness, and the unknown. You could develop a lifestyle of few risks and little uncertainty, and you would have less anxiety. But you would be bored. To enjoy life and be in the flow, you need a certain amount of uncertainty. Without some uncertainty life becomes flat and monotonous.

Explorers see the unknown as a way of life. They have no idea what lies beyond the ocean, over the mountain, across the river, or beyond the sun. But they have faith in themselves and in their abilities and in their vision. They set out, and even if they don't reach the land of their original destination, they always discover something,

Learn to develop the faith of an explorer. Your anxiety is due to lack of faith in yourself and in the world. You lack faith in airplanes to stay in the air, in cars to stop at red lights, in your body to function properly, and in others to act reasonably.

If you have public speaking anxiety you may lack faith in the audience's ability to understand you, or in your own ability to speak, or to handle questions. You may have a general lack of faith in yourself and in your ability to face adversity ("What if someone disagrees with me and asks a pointed question?"). With self-faith, you overcome your fears, and this in turn communicates your authoritativeness to your audience.

When you lack faith in others, you feel compelled to take on responsibility for their actions and feelings. You lack faith in their abilities to take care of themselves ("My son hasn't called. I'm worried about him because he's a poor driver"). You also lack faith in others' ability to relate to you ("The audience will never understand my speech") or to do their jobs ("All airplane mechanics are careless"). When you learn to have faith in yourself, you begin to have faith in others.

Across the river, beyond the sun

You develop faith through knowing. The Chinese have a saying, "What is difficult is not known; what is known is not difficult." You might rephrase it: "What is fearful is not known; what is known is not as fearful." When you get to know what frightens you—when you make friends with it—your fear, not your respect, disappears. When you know something, you no longer expect the worst.

You probably can think of many objects and events of which you think you should be frightened. If nothing else, you should be frightened of electricity and poisonous snakes, right?

Yet, electricians, who work around electricity all the time, are not frightened by it. They respect it, but they do not fear it. Their secret: They know all about it. Zookeepers are not afraid of the poisonous snakes, even though they work around them every day. They knew what the dangers are, what their own capabilities are, and how to avoid a potentially fatal bite.

Mastery: making the unknown known

Nearly all positive experiences in life have some link to mastery. Longevity, for example, has been attributed to a sense of mastery. Mastery is something you develop, not a set of skills that you are born with. People have talents in different areas, but everyone can have mastery experiences. Mastery is how you develop faith, how you make the unknown known, how you disprove the idea that you are helpless, how you eliminate anxiety

When you do something for the first time, you're usually scared. That makes sense. You lack mastery in that area. To learn to deal with new challenges with a manageable amount of anxiety, you need to learn to trust that your action (deciding to do the new activity) will lead to self-confidence, which will lead to faith. If you stay in the water long enough, you will learn to swim. Your fear of water will vanish. But if you refuse to go into the water at all, your fear will not only remain, but will also grow.

Building mastery

Learning self-faith is like constructing a building. Stone by stone, board by board, the building grows into a house, school, or cathedral. Mastery experiences are your building stones—the material with which you construct your self-faith.

The spirit

Take the offensive when you face the unknown. Much of life involves confronting and conflicting with others. Your opponent may be an official of the bank that lost your check, a graduate school adviser blocking your path toward your degree, a boss who constantly criticizes, or a teenager who manipulates you. Once you accept the reality that you are in an advocacy situation-if not in an outright battle-your options become clear. You have to face the opponent.

When you take the offensive, you make the unknown more quickly known. What you know has no power over you. You can take the offensive in many ways: introduce yourself, make the first call, overwhelm the other person with kindness, expand out rather than constrict in. Your anxiety wants to convince you of your helplessness in the face of imaginary danger. Don't let it. Letting go of your anxiety and creating self-faith is a skill like any other skill. It is something that you can do now, and with practice, you can master it.

A SUGGESTION ON HOW TO READ NEWS ARTICLES AND BOOKS

There are four concepts that one should be aware of when reading, in order to help put knowledge into perspective.

1. What is the level of abstraction that is being presented in the work? When this characteristic, or attribute, is being considered, it is not a matter of what is right, or wrong. There is no right or wrong here. There is only the perspective that is being presented. We can accept high, or low, levels of abstraction; it is only important that you understand the level that is being presented. If one is reading Plato, the information is being presented at a high level of abstraction ("It is the unexamined life that is a waste." Everything has a "primary form" that is inseparable from the object). These are high-level abstractions, and as such, can have almost an indefinite number of interpretations. The higher the level of abstraction, the harder it is to get agreement. This is why there are over 4,000 Christian denominations in the U.S, and over 24,000 in the world. Everyone thinks his or her interpretation is the correct one. Since there is no way to prove a highly abstract phenomenon, it is not likely there will ever be a consensus. (This dilemma is what is behind the Catholic Church proclamation that it is the only true church. Unfortunately for the Church, Luther didn't quite buy that directive at the same level of abstraction that the church wanted.) At the other end of abstraction, individuals like Watson, BJ Skinner, Pavlov deal with things at the experiential level. Essentially, the premise at this end of the pole of abstraction

is the point of view that all understanding can be accomplished simply by observing behavior. They believe that no real benefit can be accomplished through inserting consciousness onto an event. This is reasoning at a low level of abstraction. There can be studies done that will give credence to the observations. One can study things like what is the amount of weight that has to be added to hand one, before it is perceived as being heavier than the other hand. Or, how much louder does a sound have to be in order for it to be perceived as louder than a previous sound. These are measurable and are found to be consistent and repeatable. Is one of these perspectives more accurate than another? No. There are different levels of abstraction through which we examine similar events.

Let me give an example: If you are in a room, look around and see how many places in the room could be considered places to sit. It is likely that there would be a high agreement if 10-20 people were asked the same question. Now, let's ask a question of higher abstraction, Which of the places to sit constitute a "good" place to sit?" Now we may find the level of agreement begins to show cracks. Different people will interpret "good" in different ways, so the concordance is not going to be as high. Let's move up the pole to a question of, "What is the 'best' seat in the room?" At this level of abstraction, we might not have any agreement at all. Each person, for his or her own reasons, might see a different seat as the "best" place to sit. If we understand the level of abstraction, we will have a good idea as to the level of agreement we can expect to get among critics, students, educators, etc.

2. A second thing that should be considered when reading something is whether the person is using physical world language (change, time, effort, special knowledge, and stability), or psychological world language (no change, no time element, no stability, choice, movement, and selection) language. Is the writer consistent, or does he/she switch back and forth between the languages. The

more a person switches back and forth the more confusion there will be in the message that is being presented.

3. The third area of assessment has to do with whether the author is writing from within a childhood system of thinking that "Others are responsible for my thoughts, feelings, and actions, and I am responsible for other's thoughts, feelings, and actions (I call this System One thinking, because it is the first, or earliest, thought process we structure our life around), or whether the author is writing from the perspective of System Two thinking (a process of thinking that becomes available at about 12.5 years of age) which postulates that we are each responsible for our own thoughts, feelings and actions, and others are responsible for their own thoughts, feelings and actions.

If a psychologist wrote a book in which it was asserted that people must learn to be vulnerable if they want to be close with others, this writer would be attempting to help people from within system one. Since in System One thinking, person A is seen as responsible for person B's feelings, and person B is seen as responsible for person A's feelings, closeness is seen as generating vulnerability. The solution to the problem is very different if you can identify System One and System Two, and can get out of System One. No one should stay in System One, because if you get out of it and into System Two, closeness is no longer a vulnerable situation. In System Two people can get as close as they want without vulnerability.

Identifying whether a production is being written from the bias of System One, or Two, helps us understand the developmental level of the writer. System One is early childhood thinking, and it generates tremendous problems. System Two, available after twelve and a half, is far more productive, and it actually helps to resolve conflict; System One is a generator of violence and destruction at worse and major unhappiness at best. System One is the basic belief system terrorists ascribe to, and this is one of the reasons I believe, terrorists are anti-education. Education can help people learn to think for themselves, bringing at least some people into a higher level of problem solving that would tend to deplete terrorists of their supply of individuals willing to blow themselves up in states of hatred. When you understand you are creating nearly all of your experiences, it is difficult to vehemently hate others because of those experiences. The blame system, in my opinion, is responsible for more deaths than the plague.

4. The fourth perspective to watch out for is the way the writer or individual you are relating to perceives responsibility. Do they use responsibility and accountability interchangeably as a lawyer does, or do they separate "responsibility" (common usage) into response ability and assigned accountability? When we use these two concepts, as one concept, it can destroy people's lives (and commonly does in a court of law) where a careful separation of the concepts can lead to understanding and resolution of conflict.

If we use the concept of response ability, as the ability to respond, we learn, among other things, to know that anger is a product of our own thinking. If we don't go into blame, we do not create, or experience, anger in the first place.

Many outcomes in life are dependent on their beginnings. If we describe events and the cause of events correctly, we will believe them correctly. If we frame our understanding incorrectly, we will believe it incorrectly, and then we will act incorrectly. Say it wrong, think it wrong, and the action on the information will also be wrong.

THE DILEMMA OF BEING DELUSIONAL

In psychiatry we have thinking that is referred to as delusional. Webster II New College Dictionary 1999 defines delusion as "Something falsely disseminated or retained-Deception. A false belief held in spite of invalidating evidence especially as a symptom of certain forms of mental illness." I would hold that at a minimum of half of the world is delusional about something all the time and most likely 98% of the people in the world respond in a delusional fashion during an average day—as defined by Webster.

I will only give a couple examples here, as this could be a topic for a much larger discourse. Children believe others are responsible for their thoughts, feelings and actions. This is not an accurate perception. It is a delusion. Because children grow up, they take this belief system with them into adulthood where they continue to act delusional by claiming others are responsible for their thoughts, feelings and actions. Many parents teach this concept to their children, act as if this way of thinking is accurate, and may eventually end up in prison, when society can no longer ignore their behavior. Have you ever wondered about how so many inmates continue to claim they have done nothing wrong? It is actually fairly simple; they are delusional. They believe in the concepts that are a part of System One thinking and if you look at what they do from within that system of thinking their behaviors are logical. If I believe you have the power to make me mad, if I believe you have made me mad, it is logical for me to do something to you to impress you to stop your assault (perceived) against me. We do not label this form of delusion a mental illness, although we do label the behavior that results from this form of thinking as a mental condition: Oppositional defiant disorder, conduct disorder, episodic dyscontrol syndrome, some resulting depression and anxiety—the list goes on. Just because we all do it does not mean it is not a delusion. But, because we all do it, it is not called a delusion. If we called it a delusion, we might try to do something about it. Instead, we ignore it until it reaches an extreme point, and then we punish that person for doing what they feel.

Attorneys seem to like to work in this area of delusional thinking. An attorney in court asked me several time if I didn't feel partially responsible for his client taking a knife out of his car and then stabbing his wife and her boyfriend. I told him, "No." He continued, "Not even a little bit?" His slight of hand was to try and get the jury to buy his assessment/meaning of accountability: That I was the one responsible for his client stabbing his wife (after all that was the only way he could make a lot of money—he wanted a million dollars for each month his client was incarcerated for the deed). He was hoping by the way he asked the question that the jury might take my answer as an indication of how I didn't understand my role in the event, and how through my denial of such an "obvious" connection that he was asserting, I was just another non-caring, non-feeling, outsider who denied my responsibility for such an awful event. Fortunately, he did not convince enough of the jury, and he, and the two other attorneys, lost the assault on my attorney and me.

I would challenge the reader to define how the delusion of childhood thinking is different from the delusion of the schizophrenic. Children believe others cause their feelings, thoughts and actions. Schizophrenics believe others cause their thoughts, feelings, and actions. There are differences, but there are also similarities. The delusions of childhood are clearly initiated by an immature, developing brain system. In the average child they will develop the ability to get out of that system around 12.5 years of age. For the schizophrenic person this ability to get out of that way of thinking may not develop.

So, what prevents adults who have not given up the early way of thinking from looking schizophrenic? To some extent they do—they are both delusional. In the latter the delusions do not appear to be an amendable experience.

There is a group of people who seem to sit between the schizophrenic and the adult with a child's way of thinking. This is the people seen as "borderline personality disorder." They maintain the child's delusional position in their behavior and actions yet they can talk to you about how they know that perspective is not correct. They may want to get out of this behavior, but their "ruling principal" (term from the stoics) does not seem to allow them to do this. How are they different from schizophrenics? I think their mental issues result from experiences in childhood that served to stick them in the first belief system. Trauma acts as glue. The more of it we have the more we are stuck. If we have a lot of trauma during the time of our life when the only belief system we have access to is the blame system, it is easy to buy into the idea that others are responsible for our feelings, etc.

HOW TO PICK A THERAPIST

One of the problems with the way therapy has been taught in the past (In the present, I am not certain it is even being taught) is that problems are seen in an individual way. When this is done it opens the door to therapy interminable. The physical world keeps presenting problems for us to work out. The psychological world keeps giving us products related to the choices we make.

Psychoanalysis has certainly had its impact on people's thinking. I get people in the office all the time that will say something like "He is still angry because his parents divorced when he was in grade school. He needs to be in therapy to resolve this problem, so he isn't angry another thirty years." When a therapist buys into this type of thinking there is no end to the things that someone can muster up to be angry about over a lifetime. If the therapist understands that anger comes from blaming and teaches this to the patient, he or she may rid themselves of anger problems in 5-10 minutes of instruction, and may not have it come back in their lifetime. In the same way if a therapist tries to work with a patient on things like hurt, dissatisfaction, disapproval, jealousy, frustration, resentment, anger, communication problems, self-esteem issues, or communication issues the therapy will probably never be finished. On the other hand, if the therapist understands all of these things have a common root cause (blame system thinking) the patient can, at times, dispense with these problems in a couple weeks. I instruct my patients not to work on any of the problems mentioned above. I don't want them wasting their time and energy. These symptoms disappear when they get out of the blame system of thinking.

If you look at all of the things that have been identified as possibly causally related to suicide it would read like a dictionary. What seems to be missing on the list of causes is the one thing that is accurate: mental intermediation. Lawyers cannot make much money if we were to agree on that as a cause, so we aren't likely to run across it in the books for a few hundred more years. The current state of confusion is too lucrative.

I once did a library check on references related to suicide. I had been asked to give a talk to a school class about suicide during Suicide Prevention Week, and I was hoping to get something I could use in the talk. I got back a stack of paper about two inches high with eight or more references on each single sheet. After looking through the stack for about an hour I realized there was nothing in the entire stack that actually helped explain why people suicide. The stack of references had to do with things that were occurring in the physical world of the person who had committed suicide; whether the person was male or female, whether they were young or old, whether they had children, or no children, etc. The reference to the inside (psychological) world was usually limited to the person being either anxious or depressed. Even these observations had more to do with what was observed than what was reported. The bottom line is that the only things that explains why a person suicides is their mental intermediation at the time of the act. Because understanding this would make the person who commits suicide responsible for their act, and since that is not very lucrative idea for lawyers, it probable won't be acknowledged for some time to come.

I want to thank Gary Emery Ph.D. for his many contributions to this book.

James E. Campbell M.D

www.ingramcontent.com/pod-product-compliance
Lightning Source LLC
LaVergne TN
LVHW041811060526
838201LV00046B/1212